Analysing Media Texts

This book is part of a series published by Open University Press in association with The Open University. The complete list of books in this series is as follows:

Understanding Media: Inside Celebrity (editors: Jessica Evans and David Hesmondhalgh)
Media Audiences (editor: Marie Gillespie)
Media Production (editor: David Hesmondhalgh)
Analysing Media Texts (editors: Marie Gillespie and Jason Toynbee)

This publication forms part of an Open University course *Understanding Media* (DA204). Details of this and other Open University courses can be obtained from the Student Registration and Enquiry Service, The Open University, Milton Keynes, MK7 6YG, United Kingdom: tel. +44 (0)1908 653231, email general-enquiries@open.ac.uk.

Alternatively, you may visit The Open University website at http://www.open.ac.uk where you can learn more about the wide range of courses and packs offered at all levels by The Open University.

To purchase a selection of Open University course materials visit http://www.ouw.co.uk, or contact Open University Worldwide, Michael Young Building, Walton Hall, Milton Keynes MK7 6AA, United Kingdom for a brochure. tel. +44 (0)1908 858785; fax +44 (0)1908 858787; email ouwenq@open.ac.uk

Analysing Media Texts

Edited by Marie Gillespie and
Jason Toynbee

Open University Press
in association with The Open University

Open University Press
McGraw-Hill Education
McGraw-Hill House
Shoppenhangers Road
Maidenhead
Berkshire
England
SL6 2QL

email: enquiries@openup.co.uk
world wide web: www.openup.co.uk

and Two Penn Plaza, New York, NY 10121-2289, USA

First published 2006

A catalogue record of this book is available from the British Library

ISBN 0 335 21887 3 (hb) 0 335 21886 5 (pb)

Library of Congress Cataloguing-in-Publication Data

CIP data applied for

Edited and designed by The Open University.

Typeset in India by Alden Prepress Services, Chennai

Printed and bound in the United Kingdom by The Alden Group, Oxford.

1.1

Contents

Series preface

Analysing Media Texts is the fourth of four books in a series, entitled *Understanding Media*. The aim of the series is to provide a cogent and wide-ranging introduction to the study of the media. These four books form the central part of an Open University course with the same title (course code DA204). Each volume is self-contained and can be studied on its own, or as part of a wide range of courses in universities and colleges.

The four books in this series are as follows:

Understanding Media: Inside Celebrity, edited by Jessica Evans and David Hesmondhalgh

Media Audiences, edited by Marie Gillespie

Media Production, edited by David Hesmondhalgh

Analysing Media Texts, edited by Marie Gillespie and Jason Toynbee (with DVD-ROM)

The first book introduces four elements central to any investigation of the media (history, texts, production and audiences) via an analysis of the important media phenomenon of celebrity. The next three books in the series then examine texts, production and audiences in greater detail. Across these different topics, the course addresses three *themes* in media analysis, which the course team believe are fundamental to any appreciation of the importance and complexity of the media. These are

- power
- change and continuity
- knowledge, values and beliefs

These elements and themes can be traced via the index of each book, but the book introductions and conclusions will also help follow how they are pursued across the series.

Understanding Media covers a great deal of media studies curriculum, but of course it still isn't possible for us to cover everything. Nevertheless we have aimed to cover a wide range of media examples, both historically and geographically, and to introduce a number of differing and often competing approaches.

The chapters are designed to be rigorous but student-friendly, and we have sought to achieve this in a number of ways. We have provided clear outlines of the aims of each chapter at its beginning, and summaries at the end, with careful explanations along the way. Activities are built into the chapters, and are designed to help readers understand and retain the key concepts of the course. Just under half of these activities are based around *readings* – extracts drawn from books, academic articles and the media themselves – which are integral to the discussion contained in the chapter. These readings are indicated by a coloured line next to the margin. Each book is thoroughly indexed, so that key concepts can be tracked across the different books in the series. Further reading is indicated at the end of each chapter. Finally, although each book is self-contained, references to other books in the series are indicated by the use of bold type.

Media studies has taken its place as a familiar academic discipline in schools and universities, embraced in large numbers by students, but crassly dismissed by commentators who in most cases seem never to have read a serious analysis of the media. The need to think carefully about the media's role in modern societies is as great as ever. We hope that you find these books a stimulating introduction to this vitally important area of study.

Open University courses are produced by course teams. These teams include academic authors, from The Open University and from other institutions, experienced tutors, External Assessors, editors, designers, audio and video producers, administrators and secretaries. The Open University academics on the *Understanding Media* course team were based mainly in the Sociology discipline, within the Faculty of Social Sciences, but we also drew upon the expertise of colleagues in the Faculty of Arts, in order to construct a course with interdisciplinary foundations and appeal. While book editors have had primary responsibility for each book, the assignment of editors' names to books cannot adequately convey the collective nature of production at The Open University. The names of the *Understanding Media* course team are listed at the front of this book.

I'd like to thank all my colleagues on the course team for their hard work and good humour, especially Wendy Lampert, who has been a really excellent and efficient Course Manager.

David Hesmondhalgh, Course Chair
On behalf of the *Understanding Media* course team

Textual power and pleasure

Marie Gillespie and Jason Toynbee

This book and its accompanying DVD-ROM are about media texts: in other words, the programmes and films we watch, the newspapers we read and the songs we listen to. People who study the media use the word 'texts' because the varied media forms that we encounter every day are organised in a complex way, rather like a piece of writing. Media texts, that is to say, are *coded*. Their meanings do not just leap out at us, but are produced through rules or conventions rather like grammar in human language. Consider this example: in a fiction film a sequence that moves from a scene of someone getting into a car to a scene where the same person gets out, indicates that a journey has taken place. The meaning here may seem obvious but, in fact, depends on a convention that we could call the 'embarking–disembarking cut'. Coded meanings also work on a much larger scale. That there is even such a thing as a fiction film depends on a whole system of rules that govern how stories are told in sound and moving images (see Chapter 3 on narrative), and how they are classified according to subject matter, mood and audience expectations (see Chapter 2 on genre).

Why analyse media texts?

To some extent, analysing how media texts work echoes our everyday experiences of the media. One of the pleasures of going to the cinema or watching television is talking about the film or programme afterwards with friends or family. We take pleasure in discussing the different elements – the story, the acting, the dialogue, sometimes even the camerawork and special effects. And we pass judgements, of course. Actually, we often disagree in our judgements about the meaning of a character's action, the plausibility or realism of the story, the nature of the story's resolution or some other element of a film or programme. In doing so we may well be influenced by critics, who are paid for interpreting and judging media texts.

Of course, as students of the media we also interpret media texts and make judgements. Yet textual analysis in media studies is very different from everyday criticism, for two main reasons. Firstly, analysis of media texts involves the analysis of their structure. Unpicking structure means having a theory of that structure, a model of how conventions work together to produce meaning. In this book we examine several theoretical approaches, each of which addresses a different aspect of textual organisation: semiotics, genre, narrative and discourse. Together they make up a 'toolkit', which you can use to analyse texts.

The main aim of this toolkit is to explore the three main themes of the book separately and in relation to one another. Analysing media texts helps us understand the *power* of texts: the ways in which power relations are encoded in texts and how texts exert power over us and in society. Part of that power comes from the ways in which media texts represent and construct *knowledge, values and beliefs*. This is how and why texts function ideologically. Some texts endure and contribute to a stabilisation and continuity of certain meanings and messages but texts and their meanings also change over time. In analysing media texts we explore patterns of *change and continuity* in media systems of representation.

The second way in which the analysis of texts in media studies differs from everyday criticism is that evaluation hardly figures. Conversations that we have about the media tend to involve making judgements such as 'that film was fantastic' or 'what a boring record'. However, most textual analysis avoids attributing value in such a way. Partly this is a matter of objectivity. In the social sciences, more so than in the arts and humanities perhaps, it is important not to rely on our individual subjective experience, but to analyse the social world as objectively as is possible using rational criteria for organising and weighing evidence (see Chapter 4 for a discussion of this issue). The individual and subjective responses we often make about media texts do not tend to fit these criteria. Nevertheless, questions of value and of evaluation in textual analysis *are* commonly explored in media studies through examining the political or ideological values that shape or underpin a text.

Much research in the field of textual analysis deals with the way in which texts may be said to reinforce inequality through, for example, stereotyping, or the way in which we are encouraged to identify with certain characters or values that support dominant power relations of, say, class, gender, age, 'race' and ethnicity. A different strand of research shows how texts may encourage audiences to challenge power, often in ways which seem unlikely or not immediately apparent: for example, the creation of an imagined space of empowerment for women in soap operas.

We have been using the term media 'text' to emphasise the fact that media artefacts construct and express meanings (see also **Bonner, 2005**, for discussion of the term). Of course, to some extent, any object can carry meaning: a building, a T-shirt, a ship can all be interpreted as 'saying something', something beyond their immediate use, that is. What differentiates the media is that the primary function of media products is the making and taking of meaning (apart from the making and taking of profits). That said, the term 'text' is used in a very elastic way. It can apply to an individual image or can be stretched to refer to, say, a 24-part television serial. The important point is that, in the most common use of the term, media texts consist of a web of 'signs' – words and gestures, images and sounds – combined in ways that convey multiple possible meanings.

Media texts alone do not create meanings. Texts always have a context of production and of use. For a text to 'come to life', it requires a reader. Readers activate the meanings of texts. We come to media texts with sets of expectations and orientations that shape our readings, but different texts are more or less open to interpretation. Some texts may try to express a clear message or a dominant meaning. Others tend to be more open to readers creating multiple, even ambiguous, meanings. As readers, although we are active and selective in our interpretations of texts, we are also constrained by the ways in which meanings are framed by the text, as well as by the ways in which we are positioned and addressed by the text (as citizens, consumers, men or women; see **Gillespie, 2005**, Book 2 in this series). Still, our collective judgement of a text – as a cinema audience, for example – can turn a low budget film into a smash hit, or multi-million dollar 'blockbuster' into a flop at the box office. Equally, production plays a key role in the construction of meanings. What is 'built into' a text through, for example, its authors' intentions and unconscious desires or, more indirectly, through the way in which the media industry is structured (see **Hesmondhalgh, 2006**, Book 3) also needs to be considered. We might say, then, that the three 'defining moments' (text/production/audiences) in the social construction of meaning are relational – what is at stake in these media processes is a constant defining and re-articulating of the interrelationship between texts, producers and audiences.

With that important proviso in mind, it is worth thinking a bit more about the text-centred nature of this book. It asks you to focus on the 'defining moment' (the time in which meanings are defined) of the text, whether that be image, sound, language or a combination of these. It asks you to 'stop the flow' of moving images and sounds in order to look closely at how one image or 'shot' is organised, or to sharpen your ears to the media 'soundscape'. It asks you to 'think small and dig deep' – to take a media text and analyse how its different elements constitute a whole, and the various ways in which texts reflect or construct meanings. As these terms suggest, some approaches to textual analysis emphasise the mimetic properties of texts, or the text's capacity to reflect the world through the use of particular technologies that record images and sound with increasing accuracy. Other approaches foreground the ways in which media *never* simply reflect the world, but rather frame it and in so doing actively construct it. Still, whatever approach is adopted, textual analysis always involves close attention to specific media texts, and to their component elements. This focused attention to media texts is vital if we want to develop an understanding of how meaning is made.

The structure of this book

Sharpening your analytical skills will certainly enhance your knowledge of the media, and hopefully your pleasure too. But how can you do so? Over the last 30 years, a number of approaches to textual analysis have been developed in media studies that are now widely used. In this book, five approaches are outlined: semiotics (Chapter 1), genre (Chapter 2), narrative (Chapter 3), discourse analysis and content analysis (Chapter 4). In Chapter 5 some of the tools from the first four are used to address the question of 'textual politics' or the ideological values that can be uncovered through studying texts. This is not an exhaustive discussion; there are other approaches that we do not have space to present, and some of the techniques we discuss overlap with others. But in our view, the five approaches under consideration here provide a powerful basis for conducting systematic and theoretically informed analyses of how media texts make and convey potential meanings to audiences. How are these issues investigated in the chapters?

The first chapter, by Jostein Gripsrud, deals with perhaps the most influential approach to textual analysis in media studies, that associated with semiology or semiotics (see also **Bonner, 2005**, for an introduction to this terrain). As Gripsrud shows, semiotics is an attempt to explain how meaning comes to be made in contemporary media cultures, through a theory of signs. Signs are the building blocks of meaning. Crucially, our understandings of signs are established in accordance with social and cultural conventions. Indeed, the notion of the code-governed text (which we discussed in the first paragraph of this Introduction) comes directly from semiotics. This is, then, an approach that focuses on socially derived meaning carried in the text itself, rather than, say, the supposed intentions of the author or of the various people involved in media production. It provides not only a means of analysing texts, but also a theory of how meanings circulate and operate in society. It is for this reason that semiotics has been so hugely important in media studies. In an important sense, this approach underpins all the others sketched out in the book.

As Gripsrud suggests, however, fundamental to semiotics, and indeed to textual analysis more generally, is the notion of genre. This concept is explored in more detail in Chapter 2, by Gill Branston. One very important way in which we get an initial orientation towards interpreting texts in our everyday lives is by making sense of them as parts of wider groups, or types, of text. Genre is the French word for a 'type'. But the apparently simple act of recognition suggested here is linked to an important set of debates about how different types of texts are classified. Classification involves hierarchies of value and, as Gill Branston shows, questions about social systems of status and value are inherently political and thus never far away in textual analysis.

A third set of techniques of textual analysis treats texts as stories. Stories are fundamental to many media texts, and narrative analysis helps to raise awareness of the way in which stories structure the meanings and experiences of films, television programmes, and so on. Techniques of narrative analysis are explored by Marie Gillespie in Chapter 3. As with semiotic analysis, much of the emphasis here is on uncovering structures and conventions (shared understandings) that are not apparent in our everyday interactions with the media. But the chapter also shows how narrative conventions can only 'work' as part of a process in which the listener, reader or spectator is actively engaged.

Chapter 4, by David Hesmondhalgh, outlines two contrasting, yet related, techniques: critical discourse analysis and content analysis. Critical discourse analysis (CDA) deals with the written and spoken word. But it is not concerned with grammar so much as with the way in which language in the media produces meaning that supports dominant interests and groups in society. Hence the term 'critical': CDA is a way of analysing how texts can systematically carry meanings in ways that are not immediately apparent. CDA as a technique of textual analysis can clearly demonstrate, for example, how racism, ageism or sexism may be embodied in a particular form of words in a newspaper article or television news report. Content analysis (CA) is concerned with counting particular themes, values, images or words that may be identified in a set of texts. It is not critical per se, but can certainly be applied in a critical way. Using its techniques we could, say, count how much sexist discourse there may be in the popular press. The two approaches are differentiated partly by their difference in methodology, with CDA tending to be based on the interpretation of language use and meaning in a narrow range of texts by the analyst (interpretivist approach) and CA based on the more scientific, statistical analysis of a much wider sample of media content (positivist approach). The chapter explains these important ways of thinking about method too.

If Chapter 4 emphasises that all may not be as it seems in media texts, Chapter 5, by Jason Toynbee, examines some reasons why this might be so. Starting from the implicit claim of some texts to depict the social world realistically, it outlines key arguments in media studies about the status of the knowledge, values and beliefs we derive from the media. Can media texts tell us about the real world? And if they can, how is it that the media sometimes distort or mask the nature of society and its inequalities? One answer is that media texts may be ideological, that they imperceptibly call people into their realm of illusion in the interest of power. A more recent approach in media studies, constructionism, suggests that there is no reality that exists independently of the symbolic systems (language, images, etc.) that we use to make sense of the world. Therefore, the world we know is constructed through the symbolic systems that shape our fundamental perceptions of the way things are.

We said at the start that one way in which textual analysis differed from everyday criticism was in its use of theory. Now perhaps it is clearer what we mean. The text is clearly something that cannot be taken for granted. Rather, its character may be profoundly different according to the way you look at it, according to the set of ideas that you bring to it. And that is why we are producing this book – because we believe that textual analysis can really enrich your understanding of the media and of the world derived from its many millions of texts.

Crucially, the accompanying DVD-ROM (also entitled *Analysing Media Texts*) should enhance that understanding in a new and exciting way. The disc has five sets of interactivities, corresponding to the five book chapters. You can dip into these in any order and at any time, though Chapter 1 guides you through using the DVD-ROM, explaining its navigation and introducing the various elements – so this is the best place to start. You will probably find it most productive to begin each set after reading the relevant chapter, as the activities for each chapter build on the knowledge that you have acquired through reading the chapter and ask you to put that knowledge into practice. In this way you can become an active media analyst. You can build up your confidence and skills in tackling the analysis of very different kinds of texts: from a sitcom to a newspaper article or a short film. The DVD-ROM gives you a real opportunity to test and apply what you are learning to a range of classic and contemporary media examples in a lively and compelling way. The book and DVD-ROM refer to a number of 'key texts', which we have selected in order to reflect a range of genres. The function of the key texts is to provide a series of focal points for you, and to help to demonstrate how the different approaches to textual analysis illuminate different aspects of any given text. This will help you compare and contrast the value and outcomes of using different approaches. Perhaps the most significant 'key text' that we use across the book is the film *Imitation of Life*, directed by Douglas Sirk and first screened in 1959. We chose this classic Hollywood melodrama as a kind of textual centre-point not only because we think it is an intrinsically rich and enjoyable text to study but also because analysing it over 50 years after its release provides a historical distance that enables us to see continuities and change in how 'classic' narrative films are organised. Other examples include excerpts from the BBC sitcom *The Royle Family*, the television chat show *Trisha Goddard*, a BBC 1 Radio breakfast show, an evening news bulletin, and a range of press articles. The DVD-ROM has a 'clips gallery' called the Viewing Room, which contains extracts or pages from the 'key texts' that are discussed in the case studies throughout the book. You can view the clips and extracts in the Viewing Room at any time. These and other examples of analysis provide a basis from which you can begin to approach any media text and apply carefully honed skills and insight. We hope that doing this will enable you to produce and share knowledge about how texts organise and convey meanings, and of the social and political consequences of the fact that some meanings take priority over others.

There is also an interactive sequence-building activity that enables you put together your own short narrative from a selection of images and sounds. In this activity you shift from being a media analyst to being a storyteller. You can create a comedy, a thriller or even a comedy-thriller sequence. This is an enjoyable way of bringing together and applying key concepts from across the book and it is best done as the final activity. After selecting the shot, you can determine its length and its transition to the next shot. You can also add dialogue, music and sound effects to create particular effects – curiosity, suspense or surprise. This will give you a real taste of the creative decision making that goes into producing media texts. However, our ultimate aim here is to get you to reflect on the consequences of the decision-making process on texts and their meanings rather than turn you into a media producer – nevertheless this could well become an unintended consequence!

References

Bonner, F. (2005) 'The celebrity in the text' in Evans, J. and Hesmondhalgh, D. (eds) *Understanding Media: Inside Celebrity*, Maidenhead, Open University Press/The Open University (Book 1 in this series).

Gillespie, M. (ed.) (2005) *Media Audiences*, Maidenhead, Open University Press/The Open University (Book 2 in this series).

Hesmondhalgh, D. (ed.) (2006) *Media Production*, Maidenhead, Open University Press/The Open University (Book 3 in this series).

Semiotics: signs, codes and cultures

Jostein Gripsrud
(adapted by Jason Toynbee and David Hesmondhalgh)

Chapter 1

Contents

1 Introduction: the railway model of communication

This chapter aims to explain the important theory of communication called semiotics. Along the way it introduces key concepts that you will encounter when using semiotic theory, and shows how these can be applied in the analysis of a wide variety of media texts, from single words to television news reports and films. Semiotics, as we shall see, is an important topic in its own right, but it is also extremely helpful to know about because it underpins other approaches to textual analysis, including the ones discussed in later chapters in this book.

Most people who have gone through elementary school will be familiar with the simple, basic model of communication: SENDER – MESSAGE – RECEIVER. 'Communication' is what goes on when a 'sender' sends a 'message' to a 'receiver'. This *linear model* contains the three most important elements in all forms of communication. It also indicates the *direction* of the process. It is logically valid, but it is very simple. One could call it the railway model of communication. The railway is, as we all know, also a way of communicating.

When a place is said to have 'good communications' it does not necessarily mean that people there discuss things in an agreeable or meaningful way; it means that the place is well connected to other places by way of roads, railways, flights or ferries. This simple, linear model of communication actually compares the communication of writing, sound and pictures to the transportation of a parcel by rail. The parcel that someone wraps and posts will usually arrive safely and unchanged to the addressee, who will know exactly what to do with the contents.

However, this is not necessarily the case when the media do the transporting and when the parcels are various types of texts. In fact most of the time the media do not communicate simple, unambiguous 'information' such as 'the time is now 6.30 p.m.' Such messages can easily be transformed into 'yes' or 'no' types of questions: they are either true or false. But what is the meaning of the little video vignette that opens the main newscast every evening? When Tony Blair or George W. Bush appear on the television screen, do their pictures mean the same to all viewers? What about the direct, interpersonal communication between people in everyday life? Even the most common of sentences, such as 'the weather is pretty good today' or 'I love you when you are like this' can be more or less enigmatic depending on how they are expressed.

Both interpersonal and media communication are therefore a lot more complicated than the transport of parcels by railway. As a consequence, we need a more complex understanding of what goes on. Of course, in everyday life we do feel we understand most of what is said both in the media and among people we meet. The present chapter addresses this paradox. It shows how both the complexity and the apparent obviousness of communication can be at least partially explained by a *theory of signs*, or *semiotics* (from the Greek *semeion*, sign).

We begin, in Section 2, by examining the way in which signs circulate in everyday life. Through immersion in culture, humans have come to have a sophisticated understanding of signs, whether in language, music or visual images. This cultural knowledge takes the form of sets of codes (or rules) according to which particular signifiers (for example, the word 'dog') are associated with particular signifieds (in this example, the concept of dog). In Section 3 we focus on language, which is what semiotics was first developed to explain. We see how Saussure treated language as a sign system and argued that, in language, words gain their meaning from their relationship to and difference from each other rather than by any intrinsic relationship to the thing for which they are a sign. So, in language, as in other sign systems, meaning is constituted by difference.

So, for example, the word 'dog' means dog because of its unique arrangement of sounds. If we make a small difference, and substitute a 'b' sound for the 'd' sound, then the meaning changes completely: 'dog' becomes 'bog' and a whole new meaning is created. Section 4, then, further examines the way in which difference within sign systems is organised – namely along two dimensions, the syntagmatic and the paradigmatic. Again, language is the model here, and yet again the same basic principles can be applied to other kinds of sign such as visual images.

In Section 5 we switch to a slightly different approach, the semiotics of C.S. Peirce. Peirce distinguishes between three types of sign and we examine each of these, taking photography as a case study. The apparent immediacy of a photograph (at first sight it seems to carry its message to us just like a train) actually raises important questions about how signs work, and how far they can be said to represent reality. These issues are followed up in Section 6 in which we examine how different semiotic systems work together. In newspapers, for example, captions next to photographs 'anchor' the photographs, cueing us to a specific meaning, which might not have been apparent in the case of the image on its own (see also **Bonner 2005**, especially Figure 2.1). Finally, in Section 7, we look at the way in which semiotics can open up questions of interpretation, how it is that different people can interpret signs differently and how ambiguity is virtually 'built into' media texts of all kinds.

A last word before the chapter gets under way: semiotics can seem quite difficult if you haven't come across the subject before. But the key point to remember is that, although it involves quite a radical way of thinking about texts and meaning, it is not complicated. You just have to keep your mind open to some new concepts, and put to one side (for the time being) certain common-sense notions of how meaning is made.

2   The cultural competence of everyday life: signs and codes

Activity 1.1

Imagine turning on the television and the first thing you see are the opening credits of a news bulletin. What makes you think this is the news?   ■■■

Most readers will spend about one second deciding it is a news programme. In the case of the *BBC Ten O'Clock News* (see Figure 1.1), the animated graphic shows a view of the world surrounded by swirling rings of red and thin, white circles. This could, perhaps, be the opening sequence in a science film, or a programme about world travel. But the image is strangely abstract, which does not fit with either of these. What immediately cues us to the fact that we are watching the news is not a visual factor, but the soundtrack. Its most prominent aspects are a regular ringing tone, related to the chimes of a clock, and a drum tattoo of a rather military character. This is a kind of music we have learned to associate with matters of importance, and in particular that type of

Figure 1.1 *The opening credits of the* BBC Ten O'Clock News *use signs that, without any further explanation, tell us a great deal about what to expect from the programme*
Source: *BBC Ten O'Clock News*

programme called the news, which is presented promptly on the hour or fraction of the hour. Hearing the music, then, points us strongly in the direction of interpreting what is on the screen: not science fiction, not travel – but the *news*.

In just a second or two, then, reasonably competent film and television viewers will have 'read' what sort of programme this is from the picture and the sound. It is worth mentioning that the word for 'read' in German, *lesen*, and in French, *lire*, both are etymologically ('etymology' – the history of words) derived from the Latin *legere*, meaning the putting together of diverse elements to form a new whole. This is basically what we do when we read – we put together letters to form words, and words to form more or less meaningful sentences. But as we have just seen, a similar process takes place with pictures and sounds. We see a graphic representation of the world and abstract shapes around it. We link this to a notion of 'important world affairs'. We hear a soundtrack with a clock-like chime and a 'military' drum pattern. We link this to the idea of urgency and timeliness. Of course, these elements can mean different things on their own, but brought together they represent (because we have learned this over time) a factual genre, called the news.

Study note *You will find a video clip that shows the opening credits of* BBC Ten O'Clock News *in the Viewing Room on the DVD-ROM,* Analysing Media Texts. *You can go to the Viewing Room at any time you wish to view this and other clips discussed throughout the book.*

Each of these visual and sound elements can thus be said to function as 'signs'. According to the Swiss linguist Ferdinand de Saussure (1857–1913), who coined the term 'semiology', a sign consists of a *material signifier* and an *immaterial signified*. (It is worth noting that the term 'semiotics' is now used more frequently than 'semiology' – see Section 5.) The signifier can thus be dots, lines, shapes, sound waves or another physical, concrete entity, which we link to or associate with some idea or notion. This idea is the signified. It is notable that we hardly ever stop to think about such associative connections, since they are established in accordance with a 'code' or rule that we learned long ago. These rules are not in any book of law. They are *conventions*, that is to say 'agreements' established by way of habit in a community of users of the same language, the same sorts of pictures, music, and so on. *A code is a convention that associates a signifier with a certain signified or meaning.*

2.1 The relations between signifiers and signifieds: arbitrariness and motivation

As a consequence of being a linguist, Ferdinand de Saussure was primarily interested in speech and writing; that is, in verbal language rather than visual signs. One of the things that characterises verbal language in comparison to pictures is that the relation between signifiers and signifieds is accidental or *arbitrary*. There is nothing about actual dogs that determines that the sound 'dog' is used to refer to them. This is why the animal in question can be called *Hund* in German and *chien* in French: same animal, different words. Some small children may, at pre-school age, wonder why 'hill' is not called 'butter' and why the plants we climb are called 'trees' and not 'ball'. The simple answer, of course, is that this is just the way it is. It is something speakers of English somehow agreed upon (established a convention on) a very, very long time ago. There is in principle nothing to prevent us from shifting to call cats 'dogs' and dogs 'cats' as of tomorrow. ('But wouldn't it confuse the animals?', the hero of David Lodge's novel *Small World* (Lodge, 1985) asked when he heard the previous sentence concluding a brief introduction to semiological thinking.)

Visual signs are different. If on the television screen we see some shape that looks like a dog, we might say that what we see is a signifier that refers to the signified 'dog'. This visual sign has a very specific meaning, that of the particular dog we see. In contrast, the signifier 'dog' in the sentence 'the dog came running across the lawn' at least initially has no meaning other than a general 'dogness' attached to it: no particular breed and certainly no name. So, in language the meaning is general, while the visual dog sign on the screen is far more specific. Certainly that is the case as long as we are talking about a photographic sign or a 'realistic' drawing; a dog here will always be a collie (Lassie, perhaps?) or a German shepherd (could it be Rin-Tin-Tin?) or some other breed. Now, although this might at first suggest that photographs and realistic drawings are uncoded, that they are simply copies of things, certain media theorists would argue that they are indeed coded signs. Photographs and realistic drawings are also shaped, the argument goes, in accordance with the conventions that we follow; that is, in accordance with certain rules for the interpretation of visual or other sensory impressions that we routinely use in everyday life, and that may not be shared by all cultures. For example, a photograph of a dog might not be known in cultures where the 'dog' phenomenon is unknown – wherever that may be. As soon as one leaves photography and the most 'realistic' of drawings and paintings, it becomes even clearer that visual signs are based on codes, just as much as language is.

Consider, for example, a circle with scattered lines stretching outwards around it. This is a conventional representation or sign for the sun. We accept that the figure means 'sun' in children's drawings, for instance, even if the sun does not actually look like that when one looks at it in the sky. The same applies to all simple drawings and other stylised, more or less abstract visual forms, such as road signs and the signs on the doors of public toilets that are to inform us whether they are intended for men or women. The latter do not resemble real men and women very much, but we recognise them precisely as conventional signs for the sexes that are also sort of human-like shapes and thus partly motivated. By 'motivated' we mean simply that there is some aspect or aspects of the signifier which correspond to the signified (see Figure 1.2).

Figure 1.2 *Schematic drawings of the sun, a road sign, and symbols for men and women as used on public toilets. Although it is possible to see these signifiers as conventional (the shape of the man and woman is not totally realistic), there is also a motivational aspect to them (they are more or less the shape of men and women)*

The relations between signifier and signifieds in signs can, in other words, be *more or less conventional, more or less motivated* – from the totally arbitrary and consequently conventional in verbal language to the minimally arbitrary or clearly motivated in straightforward photography. We will return to this in a slightly different context below.

Study note *To help your understanding of the arbitrary–motivated distinction, work through the first of the Semiotics Activities in the Chapter Activities area of the DVD-ROM, Analysing Media Texts, which focuses on this issue.*

2.2 The two steps of signification: denotation and connotation

You may have noticed that, in our description of the video still from the opening credits of the *BBC News At Ten O'Clock* above, we tried to signal how an audience in effect perceives what the screen shows – the signifiers – in two steps. We first identify the world, and we then link or associate this phenomenon with important events: global significance or the like. We first see that the world is a graphic image, and then we link or associate this with the news. Such a sequence is, however, not really noticeable in real life. It is primarily an *analytical*, *logical* or *theoretical distinction* between two sorts of signification; in reality we perceive both meanings more or less simultaneously. The first of the two meanings, the immediate and direct one, is in the semiological theoretical tradition based on Saussure's work, called *denotation*; the second, 'indirect' meaning is called *connotation*. Con-notation (cf. *chili con carne* – literally, chili *with* meat) is a 'with-meaning', an additional meaning that is clinging to the first.

The scholar who developed these concepts was the Danish linguist Louis Hjelmslev (1899–1965) who, between the First and Second World Wars, further developed the 'structural linguistics' that Saussure was trying to establish as a foundation for a more general semiology. This general semiology would study 'the life of signs within society', as Saussure once put it (Saussure, 1974, p.16). The French literary scholar and cultural critic Roland Barthes (1915–1980) was then important in showing how the distinction between denotation and connotation was central in all kinds of media texts, from films to newspaper advertisements. Crucially, it was Barthes who began to apply the semiological approach to the analysis of visual images.

An important part of the reason why the distinction between denotation and connotation has been developed, is the fact that the meanings or signifieds of signs tend to change with time and place. They are not absolutely and finally fixed in their meaning once and for all. The same signifier can mean different things for different people at different times in different locations. Signs that once had positive connotations, for example, can at a later time have negative connotations. Certain symbols related to the Vikings were, for instance, commonly regarded as having positive meanings 'attached' to them in the Scandinavian countries in the 1920s. However, since Nazi organisations used them before and during the Second World War, it is now impossible to see them without having the connotation 'Nazi' present at the same time (see Figure 1.3). From a totally different area, one could think of how the 'glamrock' star Gary Glitter stood (in his platform heels, see Figure 1.4 a) for a sort of 1970s innocence – until he was convicted of downloading child pornography (see Figure 1.4b). Or one could consider how the traditional imagery of trade union solidarity (muscular men and heavy industry) may appear in a less positive light after the impact of feminism, Thatcherism and the so-called new economy. In fashion, one can very easily notice such changes in connotations over time. Clothes, shoes and haircuts that once connoted an attractive lifestyle now signify something backwards, 'hick' or stupid. Platform shoes were the thing to wear in the 1970s, looked incredibly naff for almost 20 years and then returned in the late 1990s as the preferred footwear for millions of young women.

We can also illustrate the significance of the distinction between denotation and connotation by looking at the visual signs that represent (signify) certain nation states. Take the 'American Eagle' (see Figure 1.5). One might wonder why the land of the prairie and the Wild West would not instead choose a cow or a horse as its animal. Eagles are not commonly seen where most Americans now live, while dogs and cats are ubiquitous. The choice of the eagle was, of course, made for certain historical reasons, similar to those that also made an eagle a visual symbol of Germany: the eagle is a bird that connotes pride, power – and a willingness to use violence if necessary in order to defend and feed itself. It is a predator. A cow is not. At a first semiotic level the figure of the eagle is a *motivated*, visual sign for a particular kind of bird – it *denotes* the kind of

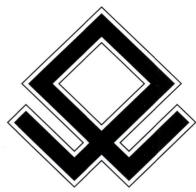

Figure 1.3 *This rune is an ancient Viking symbol that has, in more recent years, been appropriated by the Nazis. The overriding connotation of this image now is of fascism, rather than the original Viking associations with the god Odin*

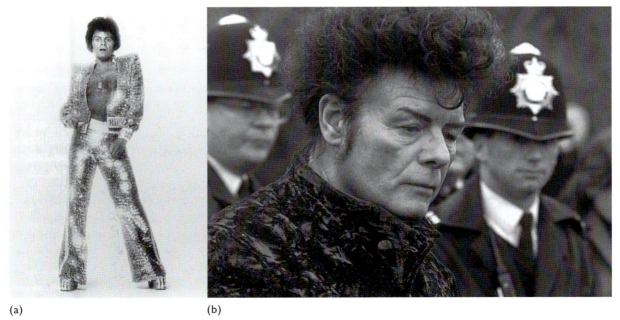

(a)   (b)

Figure 1.4 *Gary Glitter (a) in his heyday and (b) after his arrest for possession of child pornography*
Source: (a) Redferns and International Photos (b) Associated Press

Figure 1.5 *The 'American Eagle' connotes pride, power and the propensity to use violence to defend and feed itself*
Source: Corbis

bird we know as an eagle. At a second semiotic level the figure of the eagle *connotes* pride and power (and, to some, violence). In this way it can be used as an *arbitrary* or conventional symbol for the USA.

2.3 Varieties of meaning: connotational codes and cultural differences

The notion of connotative meanings demonstrates how the semiology developed by Saussure, Hjelmslev and others has been able to deal with the fact that the meanings of signs can vary according to the contexts in which they appear. That is to say, meanings are determined by the place, time and purpose of communication, and by the specificity of both senders and receivers – who it is that is sending and receiving. Signs of all sorts are always used and perceived in concrete historical, social and cultural situations and, even if most denotative meanings are more or less constant, the variation of connotative meanings is of great importance to all sorts of communication. Connotative meanings are, just as the denotative meanings, regulated by codes; in other words, the conventions that link signifiers to signifieds. However, in the case of connotation, codes are likely to be more fluid, more rapidly changing. The notion of 'code' is therefore crucial to semiology, since it is tied to certain cultural communities that share the conventions in question. *Culture* can, at least in this context, simply be defined as a *community of codes*. If one moves to a new country, it will take quite a while to get to know all the local codes, even if one may claim to 'understand the language'. Certain words, expressions, images and objects have a significance of which newcomers will be unaware. Even if one has moved to a culturally closely related country – say, from England to the USA or Canada, or from one Scandinavian country to another – one will soon notice that there are songs, names, stories and places one's new friends and neighbours know well that one has never heard of. Words one thought were quite innocent actually may cause embarrassment, perhaps because they somehow have acquired politically incorrect meanings. Thus, late-night conversations in bars or at parties may be problematic or even tiresome to follow.

Codes, and the related concept of culture, thus have important consequences not least for all sorts of international communication, both interpersonal and through mass media. Connotative codes that are peculiar to one culture can, for instance, make it hard to understand what goes on in an imported television serial. In the 1980s the Danish researcher Kim Schrøder (1988) interviewed groups of US and Danish viewers about the prime time soap opera *Dynasty* after screening a particular episode for them. He asked his interviewees to recount, among other things, the events of that episode, in which the show's 'bitch', Alexis (played by Joan Collins), who spoke with a British accent, was threatened with the line '*remember the Boston Tea Party!*' A middle-aged Danish couple remembered that there was talk about some tea party in the episode, but could not really recall that there had been any tea parties in either this episode or any other episode they had seen. So they just supposed that such an event had taken place, possibly in an episode they had missed. In other words, they lost a point that was certainly picked up by all US viewers and probably by most British as well. The Boston Tea Party was, of course, the beginning of the American War of Independence and consisted of Americans dumping a shipload of British tea into the Boston harbour. In order to understand that the line was a threat, without resorting to the tone of voice or facial expressions, one would have to know this historical reference and thus know that it connotes war against the British. One would also have to perceive that Alexis spoke with a British accent (of a sort that connotes arrogant upper classes). The Danish couple could not make these connections, and neither could most of *Dynasty*'s audiences in over 90 countries.

Knowledge of codes is often, as in this example, directly tied to factual knowledge. But it is also a vaguer sort of knowledge of conventional meanings in a certain culture. Such a knowledge depends on *familiarity* that is established through living within the culture. In

Figure 1.6 *Roland Barthes demonstrated that non-Italians have knowledge of a different set of codes for pasta products from those with which Italians themselves are familiar*
Source: Barthes, 1977/1964, plate VXII

a now classic analysis of a magazine advertisement for pasta products, Roland Barthes demonstrated how different elements in the advertisement had 'Italianness' as a shared connotation (see Figure 1.6). Barthes also pointed out how an apprehension of these signs for 'Italianness' would be dependent upon a previously established knowledge of, or familiarity with, certain tourist clichés that Italians (or Chinese, or Senegalese) do not necessarily have themselves (Barthes 1977/1964).

3   How signs gain their meaning: language as a system of differences

We can see the connections between semiology's understanding of the sign on the one hand, and notions of culture and cultural differences on the other, if we have a closer look at Saussure's theory of how signs in language actually acquire their meaning. Saussure argued that there is an arbitrary relationship between the signifier and the signified of a sign, as evidenced in the fact that different languages have very different words for the same phenomenon.

The *signifieds* divide the world into categories of 'content'. These categories, or ideas of how the world is ordered, are not always dictated by the physical realities themselves; they are often culturally specific. For instance, the colour category 'brown' does not exist in certain cultures, and the colour that we now call 'orange' did not exist a few hundred years ago. Firstly, we had the fruit 'orange', and then a couple of centuries ago its name began to be applied to a particular part of the colour spectrum, somewhere between 'yellow' and 'red'. Of course, that part of the spectrum had always existed. What changed was the fact that people began to name it and, in doing so, started to recognise it as a colour in its own right.

Along similar lines we can note that the English language has fewer words for 'snow' than the language of Inuit ('Eskimos'), while Arabic may have a particularly well-developed set of terms for camels. These are all examples of how the signifieds are to some extent culturally determined, and relatively 'arbitrarily' organised. Anthropologists are very familiar with such differences, which may even be so many and fundamental that different languages imply significantly different perceptions of the world and our existence in it.

In the 1950s the anthropologist Whorf, in co-operation with his mentor Edward Sapir, developed what is known as the *Sapir–Whorf hypothesis* or *Whorf's hypothesis of linguistic relativity* (Whorf, 1956). This hypothesis is precisely about the close connections between the way in which a language is organised and how the users of this language perceive or experience the world. The empirical basis for the hypothesis was primarily in Whorf's studies of the language of the Native American tribe the *Hopi*. This language is grammatically extremely different from European languages. It has almost no nouns, and verbs are inflected in very different ways. Such radical differences obviously make it difficult to translate from one culture to another.

3.1 How meaning is constituted through difference

Saussure argued that, since the meaning (or the signified) of a verbal sign (such as the colour 'orange') does not spring from the 'thing' (the orange colour) itself, it has to be explained as resulting from the principle that *the sign acquires its meaning through its relations to other signs* (Saussure, 1974, pp.114–20). The meaning of the verbal sign 'orange' is determined by its relations to 'red', 'yellow', 'brown', etc. The signified of a verbal sign is, in other words, determined by the opposition of its signifier to or difference from other verbal signifiers. *Language is a system of differences*. What is 'light' is determined by what is 'dark', what is 'hot' by what is 'cold'. This could be formulated as the principle that *meaning is constituted by difference*. At the level of the signifier in verbal language one can think of the way in which every word is composed of sounds that differentiate meanings, so-called phonemes. A person who lisps is fully understandable in English, but there may well be languages where a lisping 's' and a straight 's' may give otherwise similar words different meanings. To find out whether two sounds are phonemes, linguists will use a so-called permutation test. The sounds signified by 'b' and 'p' are closely related, but the difference between them is crucially important in English. One can demonstrate that by replacing the 'b' in *bass* with a 'p'. 'Pass' means something other than 'bass' and hence 'b' and 'p' are meaning-differentiating phonemes, or basic sound units, in English.

In more philosophical terms, *the role of difference in our way of thinking* has attracted a lot of attention, particularly within media and cultural studies, in the last couple of decades. Here the notion of *difference* has been central to discussions of identity (see Woodward, 1997). Since we tend to think in terms of differences, understood as *oppositions*, we also immediately think in categories. These categories tend to render quite difficult the imagining of gradual transitions, in-between things or states and any interconnections between the two poles of an opposition. The fundamental example is the opposition between male and female, which, through enormous networks of connotations, is used to define anything from sexual preferences to clothes, cars, behaviour and ways of thinking. Another example could be the racial opposition between 'black' and 'white'. 'Black' here tends to cover everything that is not absolutely 'white', thus radically polarising and simplifying an enormous variety of skin colours and other so-called 'racial' attributes (see **Bennett, 2005, Section 5**).

Signification through difference can also work in a more subtle way. For an example of semiotic interpretation that shows this read the following extract from Roland Barthes, 'The face of Garbo'. In it Barthes discusses the face of the Swedish actress and Hollywood star, Greta Garbo. Figure 1.7 is a still photograph from her film, *Queen Christina* (USA, dir. Mamoulian, 1933), which Barthes discusses.

Bearing in mind the discussion above of denotation, connotation and signification as a system of difference, consider the following questions and make notes as you do so:

- What, according to Barthes, does the whiteness of Garbo's face signify?
- Can you identify any binary oppositions to which Barthes might be pointing?

Reading 1.1

Roland Barthes, 'The face of Garbo'

Garbo still belongs to that moment in cinema when capturing the human face still plunged audiences into the deepest ecstasy, when one literally lost oneself in a human image as one would in a philtre, when the face represented a kind of absolute state of the flesh, which could be neither reached nor renounced. A few years earlier the face of Valentino was causing suicides; that of Garbo still partakes of the same rule of Courtly Love, where the flesh gives rise to mystical feelings of perdition.

It is indeed an admirable face-object. In *Queen Christina*, a film which has again been shown in Paris in the last few years, the make-up has the snowy thickness of a mask: it is not a painted face, but one set in plaster, protected by the surface of the colour, not by its lineaments. Amid all this snow at once fragile and compact, the eyes alone, black like strange soft flesh, but not in the least expressive, are two faintly tremulous wounds. In spite of its extreme beauty, this face, not drawn but sculpted in something smooth and friable, that is, at once perfect and ephemeral, comes to resemble the flour-white complexion of Charlie Chaplin, the dark vegetation of his eyes, his totem-like countenance.

Now the temptation of the absolute mask (the mask of antiquity, for instance) perhaps implies less the theme of the secret (as is the case with Italian half mask) than that of an archetype of the human face. Garbo offered to one's gaze a sort of Platonic Idea of the human creature, which explains why her face is almost sexually undefined, without however leaving one in doubt. It is true that this film (in which Queen Christina is by turns a woman and a young cavalier) lends itself to this lack of differentiation; but Garbo does not perform in it any feat of transvestism; she is always herself, and carries without pretence, under her crown or her wide-brimmed hats, the same snowy solitary face. The name given to her, *the Divine,* probably aimed to convey less a superlative state of beauty than the essence of her corporeal person, descended from a heaven where all things are formed and perfected in the clearest light. She herself knew this: how many actresses have consented to let the crowd see the ominous maturing of their beauty. Not she, however; the essence was not to be degraded, her face was not to have any reality except that of its perfection, which was intellectual even more than formal. The Essence became gradually obscured, progressively veiled with dark glasses, broad hats and exiles: but it never deteriorated.

Figure 1.7 *Greta Garbo in* Queen Christina *(USA, 1933)*
Source: Kobal

Reading source
Source: Barthes, 1973, pp.62–3 ■ ■ ■

The piece was first published as one of a series of newspaper articles in the 1950s. These inaugurated a new kind of criticism of popular culture. Here, for example, by approaching the face of Garbo as a semiotic structure, Barthes was able to show the complexity and richness of Hollywood cinema, a phenomenon that most intellectuals at the time considered to be worthless mass culture. His 'cool', analytical approach pays close attention to the text, yet at the same time is strangely distant. There is no question of trying to understand the characters Garbo plays, or even empathising with a notionally real Garbo. Instead her cinematic image is read as a system of difference, one that yields a mythical, almost religious meaning of 'human perfection'. No doubt you will have identified aspects of the system: white versus black, male versus female (this difference, Barthes suggests, is actually suppressed in Garbo), and perfection versus degradation.

4 Syntagms and paradigms

Clearly, then, difference is critical for semiology. Its impact as an organising principle in social life extends all the way from letter and word up to the level of large-scale texts, and indeed questions of cultural and political difference. However, the theory of semiology does not only treat difference in terms of the kinds of binary oppositions we have been looking at – important as these are. It further proposes that difference is organised along two dimensions, those of the syntagm and the paradigm.

A syntagm is normally the same as a sentence, but one may also think of it as something more extended, as referring to the *linear dimension of a text*, its 'sequenciality'. Grammar lessons at school might have taught you that different languages have different patterns in which correct sentences are made. For example, in the place reserved for the subject of the sentence, one must place nouns, not verbs. (So, in English, we say 'the cat sat on the mat', or we could say 'the man sat the mat' but we would never say 'ran sat on the mat'.) This gives us wide, but not unlimited, sets of possibilities when constructing sentences. The categories from which we make choices when filling the designated places in the sentence pattern, can then be called *paradigms*. There are verb paradigms, adverb paradigms, and so on, that consist of all verbs, all adverbs, and so on, respectively. Paradigms may be thought of as 'storage shelves' where one finds and takes out the words one needs to fill certain places in the syntagms.

An example of the relationship between syntagms and paradigms is shown in Figure 1.8. In this figure, syntagmatic and paradigmatic dimensions correspond, respectively, to 'horizontal' and 'vertical' axes.

In Figure 1.8 the last noun of the sentence (its object – 'mat') has been used as the position at which other possible paradigms might be slotted in. But we could equally well have substituted other verbs for 'sat', other prepositions for 'on', and other nouns for 'cat'. In other words, at every link in the chain of this syntagm (as in all syntagms), paradigmatic selection is being carried out.

If we then move from grammatical analysis to a semiotic analysis of signification more generally, similar conditions apply. All sorts of signification can be thought of as organised in syntagms where the components are selected from paradigms, which here will be groups of verbal or other signs *with a similar or related meaning*. The relation could either be of the type called *parasynonymy* – that is, semi-identical meaning, as between 'warm', 'hot' and 'boiling' – or it could be of the type called *antonyms* – that is, contradictory pairs such as 'hot' versus 'cold', 'light' versus 'dark', and so on. The main thing is, according to the French film semiotician, Christian Metz, that paradigms consist of a number of units that compete for the same place in the syntagmatic chain, and that any chosen unit (word, picture, sound, etc.) gets its meaning through a comparison with those that could have appeared in the same place (Metz, 1982, p.180).

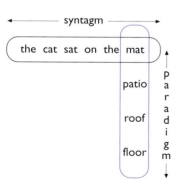

Figure 1.8 *The relationship between syntagms and paradigms*

4.1 Some examples of paradigmatic–syntagmatic relationships

The principle of syntagmatic–paradigmatic relations was central to Saussure's idea of language as a system of differences (actually Saussure used the term 'association' rather than paradigm). What is important in media and cultural studies, then, is the extension of this principle to cover *all media and forms of communication* by way of analogy. A stereotypically French example of a syntagm could be the menu at a restaurant. It is ordered in accordance with a culturally specific sequence of various types of dishes that make up a decent meal: starters, main courses, cheeses and desserts. This sequence can be regarded as a culturally specific *syntagmatic code*. If someone orders the courses served in the reverse order, this will be met with raised eyebrows at least. (In the UK, however, the cheese very often comes after the dessert in the menu order in many restaurants and in the specific ritual of port and stilton (cheese) beloved of Oxbridge colleges.) For each element in the syntagmatic chain, each course, there are paradigms from which one makes selections. Not just anything will fit as a starter, and what fits as a starter will not be found in the paradigm of desserts.

Another example could be clothing. There are paradigms for headwear, upper- and lower-body garments, socks and shoes. Wearing knickers as a hat will be a breach of a paradigmatic code – and also of a syntagmatic one. For there are syntagmatic codes for combinations: a tuxedo jacket does not fit with jogging trousers. It is a breach of the code, as is slalom boots worn with a ballroom dress. Such breaches of codes can of course be done, not least in order to draw attention. They may therefore also successfully be used in humour or advertising.

In film and television we might therefore imagine lighting, camera angles, and so on, as selected from 'storage shelves' or paradigms full of more and less adequate alternatives, and every selection will contribute to a meaning which would be changed if other selections were made. So, the idea of paradigms and syntagms can be successfully transferred from language to more visual and conceptual arenas. However, there are problems with this transfer. One problem is that words are *discrete* – that is, clearly separated entities – while selections of filmic elements such as lighting and camera angles will most often be made from continuous scales where the differences will be gradual. Still, the idea that those who make a film or any other text continuously make choices among alternatives that have consequences for the meaning of the final 'syntagm' or product is clearly both sustainable and important.

The paradigmatic dimension of texts is, then, the selection of elements for the places in the syntagmatic chain, and the relations between the selected elements and the alternatives. This is a key to the *theme* of a text; that is, what it can be said to be about at a deeper level, and how it treats its subject(s). One can, for example, think of the choice of characters for a fictional story in a particular medium. From the paradigm 'women' one can choose from a variety of possibilities, and the same is of course the case for the paradigms 'men', 'human relations', 'settings', 'conflicts', and so on. The prime-time soap *Dynasty* (which I keep referring to since I wrote a book about it – Gripsrud, 1995) had a couple of female lead characters who were clearly older than probably all other leading ladies in US prime-time television fiction – characters who were around their forties. The show therefore came to thematise women's ageing and the question of what this process is supposed to mean. When action movies have female heroes instead of the usual muscular men, they thematise the notions of femininity in our culture. In both of these examples we are talking about conscious paradigmatic choices made by the producers. The *unconscious choices* may be even more interesting, those that have been done 'automatically', since they will be related to – be indexical signs or symptoms of – norms and understandings that are so ingrained that one does not stop to think about them.

The 'character paradigm' of US soap operas was once described like this by a US critic (see Figure 1.9):

> Soap opera people belong for the most part to the socially and professionally successful. They are well-groomed and cleanly limbed. They live in homes with no visible mops or spray cans that yet wait shining and ready for any unexpected caller. At the same time, almost all of soap opera's characters are drawn from the age group that spans the late teens into middle-age. They constitute what might be called the legitimately sexually active portion of the population. And the great majority come from the generation that reaches from the mid-twenties into the mid-forties. That is to say, they suggest a sexuality that has transcended the groping awkwardness of adolescence but that never goes beyond a commerce of bodies which are personable and smooth – even the older men are clean older men.
>
> Porter, 1982, p.126

This description of the code that guides the selection of characters by the writers of US soaps obviously says something about dominant US culture. The UK code tends to provide a paradigm of characters that is

Figure 1.9 *(facing page) The differences between US and UK soap opera character paradigms are quite apparent when comparing US and UK soap operas. UK soap operas reveal a code that allows for a wide variety of types of character (a) Nick Cotton from* EastEnders *and (b) Vera Duckworth from* Coronation Street. *US soap operas, however, operate with a code that constrains their choice of characters to 'clean-cut' men and women (c) Bobby Ewing and Jenna Wade from* Dallas *and (d) Brenda Walsh, Kelly Taylor and Donna Martin from* Beverly Hills 90210
Source: (a) BBC (Nick), (b) Granada (Vera), (c) and (d) Kobal (both)

(a)

(b)

(c)

(d)

radically more inclusive in terms of looks, ages and degrees of success in life (see Figure 1.9). Paradigms such as these, and the selections made from within them, can thus often tell us something about underlying, not necessarily acknowledged, features of a society and a culture, or a way of thinking. They become *symptoms*, and a clever textual analyst may be able to formulate a diagnosis. Such analyses are therefore sometimes called *symptomatic readings*. These diagnose not so much the psyche of the individuals who created the text, as the society, culture or milieu of which they are parts and with which they share values and ideas. This issue, of perceiving shared values via textual analysis, is explored further over the course of the next four chapters.

5   The sign according to C.S. Peirce

So far in this chapter we have largely kept to the Saussurian tradition in the theory of signs; that is, semiology. The most frequently used term for the theory of signs these days, however, is *semiotics* (hence the use of this term also in this chapter's title). This term was coined by the American philosopher, physicist and mathematician Charles Saunders Peirce (1839–1914) who, independently of Saussure, had a series of related ideas. His definition of a 'sign' is different from Saussure's and he has other ideas as to the components of the sign. According to Peirce, anything that in some way or other stands for something else in some respect or capacity is a sign. It is thus already at the outset clear that Peirce (unlike Saussure) does not take verbal language as his point of departure. For Peirce, signs are something much more extensive – in fact, *everything is signs*, to the extent that everything means something to us.

Because everything is signs, a semiotics in Peirce's sense will have it that, when we see a horse at a distance of three feet, it is a horse-sign we see. We see forms and colours and may hear sounds and recognise smells that we associate with the meaning 'horse'. If we go over and touch the horse, we will perceive more signs of the same, such as soft hairs over strong muscles, a mane, and so on. If we are still in doubt, we may get some final sign-evidence when the horse kicks our behind. Peirce's semiotics is, in other words, a theory of perception and a theory of knowledge (epistemology) at least as much as it is a theory of communication. It is, moreover, radically pragmatic or context-based, in that it makes the meaning of a sign dependent both on the particular person who encounters it and the situation in which it is encountered: what is a sign for me need not be a sign for you. Thus the distinction between denotation and connotation disappears (see Section 2.2). In Peirce's view *all* signification depends on situation, including what we have been calling denotation – the apparently 'fixed' meaning of a given

sign. This can also be seen if we take a look at a
graphic representation of Peirce's model of the
components of the sign (see Figure 1.10).

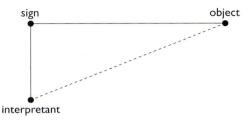

The 'sign' is that which stands for something else,
and the 'object' is that for which the sign stands. The
interpretant is the signification or meaning that the
sign has for someone. A simple, stylised drawing of
the sun may be the sign. The object is then the sun
we (sometimes) see in the sky. And our thought '[this

Figure 1.10 *Peirce's model of the sign*

is] the sun' is the interpretant. ('Interpretant' is derived from the word
interpretation, and it does not refer to the interpreter but the
interpretation.) An important point here is that the object is not the thing
itself, not 'the actual sun'. In line with the example of the horse above,
the object is also a sign; that is, certain phenomena (light in the sky, heat)
that we interpret as signs of 'the sun'. And not only is the object a sign
in its own right, the same goes for the interpretant – the word or term
'sun' in this example. The interpretant may itself result in
a new interpretant in a new triangular sign. The sign 'sun' may, for
instance, be interpreted, associated with or perceived as 'star', a radically
more distant and possibly extinguished sun. The new object will then be
'a star (in the sky)'. The term 'star', the new interpretant, may then by
some be taken to mean 'movie star' – and a series of new interpretants
is then made possible. Such processes of ever new interpretations or
signs are called *unlimited semiosis*. They may be reminiscent of how
conversations might develop at more or less festive occasions where
various associations made by participants can lead far away from the
subject that first was discussed. In media studies it may be easier to think
of how literary texts or films are interpreted again and again, including
reinterpretations of previous interpretations. In the field of political
communication one might think of how terms such as 'environmental' or
'environment friendly' have gone through similar chains of interpretants
and signs, *mediated by* or *produced by the media*.

Peirce's model of the sign, and the idea of 'unlimited semiosis', imply
that it is impossible to determine the final and absolute meaning of signs.
This way of thinking is highly dynamic; that is, orientated towards the
shifts in meanings according to specific situations and a high degree of
flexibility in the sign systems that cultures consist in – and that the media
produce and mediate. (For a critical perspective on 'unlimited semiosis',
see Chapter 5).

5.1 Peirce's three kinds of sign – and a discussion of photography's relation to reality

Peirce distinguished between three types of sign (symbol, icon and index). Whether a sign is a symbol, an icon or an index depends upon the logical relation between the sign and that for which it stands. Signs where the relation is *arbitrary* and totally *conventional* (see Section 2.1) are called *symbols*. Verbal language belongs in this category, as do the colours of traffic lights, certain logos and other phenomena for which we must learn a certain code in order to grasp the meaning. The second type of sign is called an *icon* or an iconic sign. These are signs that resemble what they stand for. They are simply pictures, or sculptures; that is, two- or three-dimensional representations of a more or less photographic or 'realistic' type (a photograph of the US President is an iconic sign for the US President). The third and last type of sign is called an *index* or indexical sign. 'Index' is the Latin and English word for the first finger, which is frequently used to point at things, and an indexical sign points at that for which it stands. It does so in the sense that there is a *causal* relation between the sign and that for which it stands. Smoke is an indexical sign that something is burning and snot indicates (is an indexical sign for) a bad cold. The symptoms doctors look for when they are to come up with a diagnosis are indexes of diseases or injuries. The clues, leads or traces that detectives look for are indexical signs for the murderous activities that they are investigating.

These categories can actually become key terms in important theoretical debates with practical consequences. Photographs, for instance, are clearly iconic signs, but whether they are also indexical has been disputed. The dispute concerns photography's status as a medium for objective documentation, a technology that delivers indisputable facts. Photography can be said to be indexical because in a sense it is a pure 'effect' of the light reflected by the object(s) in front of the camera when the picture was taken. Photography is accordingly a purely physical–chemical cause and effect system, untouched by human hands, and consequently an 'objective' representation of whatever was in front of the camera. The argument against this is that the photographer has to make a number of choices, of framing, point of view, lenses, lighting, film speed, etc. – plus all the choices in the darkroom. Put together, all of these choices provide the photographer with so much space for her or his subjectivity that photography is no more indexical than is any drawing.

This sort of scepticism about the objectivity of photography can lead to a quite provocative conclusion when the issue is whether computer-manipulated photographs in the media should be explicitly marked as such (for example, 'This photograph has been digitally manipulated'). The Danish philosopher and media scholar Sören Kjörup (1993) has, for instance, argued against such a procedure, since it would imply that the public is encouraged to regard analogue (non-digital) photographs as *not* 'manipulated', and therefore as pure and objective documentation. For Kjörup any such implication is misleading. Opponents of this position, however, make the point that in the case of analogue photography it *is* a direct physical–chemical reaction that imprints an image on the light-sensitive film. And they propose that, even if the analogue photographer has manipulative possibilities too, the physical–chemical process involved here means that photography has a documentary potential of a totally different kind than that at stake in digital photography.

The defence of the indexical character of photography is also a defence for prevailing notions of *truth* – the idea that there are certain facts, especially concerning physical reality, that are objective; that is, indisputably correct information about an objective reality that exists independently of those who study it and their approaches to it. According to this view, to present computer-manipulated pictures where the alterations done are not detectable as though they were ordinary photographs, is to tamper with notions of truth that are fundamental to modern science, politics, law and a number of other social and interpersonal domains (for more on debates over the notion of truth see Chapter 5).

This question of whether computer-manipulated photographs should be marked as such in the (journalistic) media is, then, just a small part of a larger discussion on the status of photography and photographic media in general as providers of objective representations of reality. This is obviously of central importance to the question of how we are to regard the footage and still photography that are so integral to television news, current affairs and other documentary programmes. I would for my part suggest that, even if we maintain that photographic representations are indexical signs, this does not have to mean that we believe they deliver totally objective, indisputable renditions of what went on or goes on in front of the camera. There are good reasons to sympathise with those who warn against an unproblematic faith in photography.

These issues concerning the semiotic character of texts and the relationship of texts to the real world are central in many media contexts. They also point to the importance of understanding semiotics in light of and in combination with the other perspectives on media texts that we deal with in the following chapters. It therefore seems sensible to focus on the question of photography and truth in the next two sections of this chapter.

6   Images and verbal language – relay and anchorage

Until now we have mostly talked about verbal language and images separately from each other, as though each type of sign stands on its own. However, images are composed of elements that are not as clearly distinguished as the word-signs of verbal language. The meanings of images are therefore often unclear, fleeting or plural. This is one central reason why images tend to be combined in some way with verbal language. In film and television they are accompanied by dialogue, writing (graphic signs) and/or music. Press photos are accompanied by a caption and/or an article or story. Images in advertising are accompanied by a text, at the very least the logo of the company or a trade mark. Art pictures as a rule have a title, but at times artists may wish to say that spectators can interpret their piece as they like and thus the title is in effect 'No title'. In Roland Barthes' article, 'The rhetoric of the image' (1977/1964), he distinguished between two types of function that verbal language can have in relation to images: *anchorage* and *relay*. The term 'relay' (French: *relais*) originally refers to the change of horses at posting stations in the (very) old days, but here, accordingly, it means that the text adds something that is not actually present in the image; that is, it adds some new element of meaning to the whole. A fresh horse takes over. The captions in the dialogue bubbles of comics provide a much-used example of this. Anchorage is, however, perhaps the more fundamental function. Here verbal language is used to point out which of the many possible meanings of an image are the most important. This is in a sense also what the relay function does – it draws attention to certain possible interpretations and specifies them by way of additional information. But at the same time – and Barthes overlooked this in his analysis – the image can also anchor the verbal text, that is to say influence or shape it to some degree, in some way. We shall have a look at a particular example in Activity 1.2 below (this activity also illustrates syntagms and paradigms further).

First, however, a few words of preliminary explanation. Even though relatively simple still images do not have a clear sequence in the manner of a sentence, or a scene in a film, we can nevertheless consider them as syntagms. It is just that all the elements are presented and perceived simultaneously rather than being 'unrolled' sequentially as in language. The individual elements can be thought of as having been chosen from paradigms in such a way that they form a 'sentence', statement or utterance. So, for example, the photograph in Figure 1.11 from *The Sun* newspaper can be viewed as a meaningful syntagm, one composed of the following paradigmatic elements: boy, girl, outstretched arms, conkers, goggles. We should note that this simple breakdown is not exhaustive;

it would be possible to point to many more elements. However, this is Barthes' thrust: in identifying the elements, the caption or title can put us on the track of what is being 'said' by the image. In the case of film and television, things are rather different. Verbal text that makes up the title of the film or programme will often be presented to us before we get to see the images. The images may then help us understand what an often quite enigmatic or ambiguous title is supposed to mean.

Activity 1.2

Look at the photograph with captions in Figure 1.11. Start by identifying paradigmatic elements in the photograph. You can use the list provided in the previous paragraph, but feel free to add others that you think may be significant. Now look at the captions that surround the photograph on three sides.

- What impacts do these have on what is signified by the photograph itself?
- How, if at all, does the photograph affect the signification of the captions? ■ ■ ■

You may find that doing Activity 1.2 is surprisingly difficult. Partly this has to do with the fact the much of the meaning is connotational or relies upon knowledge of vernacular English. But another factor is that what appears to be a simple message is actually complex. This is a whole ensemble of signs, all of which interact to produce meaning. Certainly there is no right answer. But some of the things you notice might include:

- The caption in small print at the bottom anchors the paradigmatic elements in the photograph, especially the conkers and masks. The pun, 'the mind goggles', contributes to this as well. Incidentally, puns work in a paradigmatic way: here 'g' is substituted for 'b' to turn 'boggles' into 'goggles' (for those of you whose first language is not English 'the mind boggles' means 'one is incredulous').

- The captions at the top and side, by ironically using the language of a public health warning or instruction manual, work to show us that children wearing masks in the playground is absurd. This is a good example of relay. The use of this style of language, as opposed to, say, journalistic description, is also a paradigmatic selection.

- Just as the words inflect the meaning of the photograph, so too the photograph of 'innocent' children points up the fact that the top and side captions are indeed ironic.

SCHOOL HEALTH WARNING

Conkers may shatter when hit by another conker. Protect eyes by wearing plastic goggles

The mind goggles . . . kids play conkers in protective masks in playground at Cummersdale School

A HEAD teacher has ordered kids to play conkers in plastic goggles — after a warning from health inspectors.

Shaun Halfpenny says he was forced to bring in the ruling to get round crazy new safety guidelines.

He bought two pairs of goggles to prevent children getting eye injuries from flying pieces of conker.

Children take it in turns to use the plastic glasses at playtime at Cummersdale Primary School in Carlisle.

Mr Halfpenny claims it was the only way he could let the kids play conkers after receiving a memo on health and

By ROBIN PERRIE

safety. He said: "The children asked to play conkers in school and I thought it would be really mean if I said no.

"I was aware of a memo that had gone round warning about health and safety related to play in school.

"These days you cannot be too careful, especially when health and safety inspectors are watching.

"At the same time this is a custom that should not die.

Many schools have banned conkers for fear of getting sued if pupils are injured.

Mr Halfpenny's move came after kids discovered a bumper crop of conkers on a school trip. He said: "I needed to make sure every-

thing was done safely. So I drilled through the conkers myself to save little hands and fingers and went out to buy two pairs of goggles.

"If anything the goggles have increased the joy in the game, it gives it a sense of occasion."

Last month council chiefs in South Shields triggered outrage when they chopped the branches off horse chestnut trees claiming it was unsafe for kids to collect conkers.

Tory MEP Martin Callanan hit out at the goggles ruling.

He said: "It's over the top. I can't remember a child ever receiving a serious eye injury from a shattering conker.

"The worst that could happen is a sharp rap to a finger."

The Sun Says — Page Eight

MORE BONKERS IDEAS

HERE are some more nutty precautions The Sun has dreamed up for kids' games:

HOPSCOTCH: Pupils must wear surgical masks so chalk dust does not cause asthma.

JACKS: Kids should wear safety helmets — like in our mock-up photo, left — in case the little ball bounces on their heads.

SKATEBOARDING: Boards should be fitted with square wheels to prevent speeding.

BRITISH BULLDOG: Catcher must be muzzled and chained to prevent injuries to others.

CATCH: Pupils to wear full body armour and helmets in case they are hit by the ball.

TAG: Playground speed cameras would stop kids running too fast. Social workers to help tagged players reintegrate afterwards.

FOOTBALL: Only soft foam balls should be used in case pupils are accidentally hit.

Figure 1.11 Relay and anchorage. Both the image and the words work in concert to tell this news story, which appeared in The Sun newspaper

Source: *The Sun,* 4 October 2004

■ Finally, you may have considered the layout and typography of
'SCHOOL HEALTH WARNING'. It is represented, iconically, as
a warning sign of the sort placed near the entrance to a building site.
The type of lettering used confirms (anchors) this interpretation. It
reinforces the ironic effect of the caption at the side. And of course
this style is a paradigmatic substitution for a more conventional
headline typography.

7 Semiotics and interpretation

A 'culture', as we saw earlier, may be defined as a *community of codes*
(Section 2.3); that is, as a set of ideas about what signs mean and how
they may be put together that is shared by a large or a small group of
people. 'Communication' is a Latin word that originally meant 'making
(something) common (or shared)'. Communion, commune, communism,
communitarianism – and, of course, common – all have the same root.
The concepts 'code', 'culture' and 'communication' are thus closely
related in many and complex ways. It should also be clear from the
discussion in this chapter that a model of communication that likens the
communication of meaning to the straightforward sending of a parcel by
train (mentioned in the chapter Introduction) cannot be used as more
than a minimal point of departure. Culture understood as a community
of codes is both a *prerequisite* of communication – as a shared condition
for the process – and a *complicating factor*. The model must be lowered
into the cultural sea of codes, to put it poetically. In addition, this sea of
codes is also surrounded by other social and material structures and
processes – institutions, technologies, markets, social classes, gender
relations, racial relations, and so on.

Semiotics – understood as a joint term for the traditions of both
Saussure and Peirce – deals with dimensions of the process of
communication that social scientific research in the field has traditionally
overlooked. This is why the sociologist Stuart Hall, then at the
Birmingham Centre for Contemporary Cultural Studies, could create a
sort of watershed in the history of media research simply by introducing
the notions of signs and codes in a famous article on encoding and
decoding (Hall, 1980, originally written in 1973). Semiotic theory is
mainly developed with a view to the understanding and analysis of texts;
that is, the entities that are 'transported' in a process of communication.
But, as we have seen, semiotics is also a highly important aspect of a
more general theory of culture. It therefore also provides a productive
approach to what goes on when the media's texts are produced as well as
when they are received, used and understood by audiences.

An important aspect of this is the way in which semiotic theory treats relations between reality outside of media texts and these texts' representations of that reality. We have already discussed how both Saussure's and Peirce's versions of semiotics render the relations between language and external reality (between signs and that to which they refer) problematic and variable. Even if photographic signs – photographs, film and video footage – can be awarded a special status as indexical signs in the sense of C.S. Peirce, semiotic theory still contributes to an understanding of the uncertainty that may well arise when one is to decide what such photographic signs actually *mean*. It is in particular the notions of 'connotation' and 'connotational codes' that can do this, since they refer to the variability of all meanings.

One example (which is of particular interest to me, as a Norwegian, but is still generally illustrating) can be taken from the soccer World Cup in France in 1998 (see Figure 1.12). In the final minutes of Norway's match against Brazil, the referee gave Norway a penalty. It was unclear to most people, both in the stadium and in front of millions of television screens, whether he had a good reason to do so, even to those of us

Figure 1.12 *The Norwegian football team celebrate after winning a match against Brazil in the 1998 World Cup in France. The referee awarded Norway the penalty that won them the match after a tackle between two players that was initially considered to have been faked. Only video footage vindicated the referee in his decision*
Source: Action Images

who had been glued to the screen when the Brazilian supposedly did something wrong. According to the English writer Julian Barnes, in *Time* magazine (Barnes, 1998), the global television audience agreed that the Norwegian player Tore André Flo just 'unexpectedly sat down', that he was just faking it when 'collapsing for no good reason'. All available footage from any camera angle and all studio experts seemed to agree that the referee was tricked and so the Norwegians were consequently 'lucky bastards' (Barnes) to win the match with the aid of the penalty, while Brazil was the victim of a fraud.

However, after 'everyone' had been talking about this for a couple of days, still according to Barnes, 'an obscure Swedish video clip' emerged that showed that Flo's shirt had actually been (illegitimately) pulled to the extent that he ended up on his behind. This saved the honour of Flo and the Norwegian team, while confidence in television's total overview and precise rendering of facts was a bit tarnished.

The interesting thing here is that the trust in television's coverage was weakened by a video clip – in which everyone, including Julian Barnes, chooses to have full confidence. And judging from this Swedish video clip, it does actually seem reasonable to argue that the penalty shot was justified. But if the Brazilians had hired a few top US lawyers, it might after a while have looked differently, at least to Brazilians and others with a reason to distrust the moral stature of Norwegian soccer players.

It is indisputable that the Swedish video clip shows that Flo's shirt is pulled by a Brazilian player so that it stands out 'like a sail', as the Norwegian coach Egil Olsen put it at the time. This was the objective, indexical signified of the photographic sign. But it was hardly this alone that resulted in the penalty. Shirt-pulling is not allowed, but it has become so common that hardly any referee in an international match at this level would blow the whistle because of it, especially not within the penalty area. The reason for the penalty was that the judge, and later everyone else, assumed that it was the shirt-pulling that suddenly had Flo sitting on the ground. Our imagined US lawyers might have claimed that the experienced professional player with the English club Chelsea had simply chosen to *pretend* that he was pulled so hard that he fell, when he just felt his shirt pulled. It would be very hard to prove them wrong from the video images alone.

The persuasive power of the video clip depends on how one perceives Flo as a player and person. To Norwegians, he is simply a great guy from the tiny village of Stryn in the fjord country, and so he has a non-photographable moral disposition that makes calculated dirty tricks unthinkable. To people from other countries, such as the referee and Julian Barnes, it may be that ideas of Norway as a peripheral, well-ordered, quite innocent and in some ways slightly backwards country (lots of nature, only four and a half million inhabitants) would have a similar effect when assumptions were to be made about Flo's morality. Interviews, and so on, with him could also have supported the assumption that this sort of country boy would not be capable of dirty tricks. These, then, were the connotative codes at work when the video clip was seen as demonstrating beyond doubt that the penalty was correct. But, as our US lawyers might have suggested, Flo could instead be regarded as an experienced, enormously wealthy player in one of the toughest soccer leagues in the world, the English soccer league, a cynical sports circus. Then the indexical document might easily appear to be dubious evidence of the correctness of the penalty, at best.

Another, and more serious example – which is also much more well known – can be taken from Los Angeles in 1991. When the African-American Rodney King was arrested in March of that year, a man by the name of George Halliday was standing nearby with his video camera, taping what went on (see Figure 1.13). He sold the tape to a local television station for US$500. This was the basis of something the US film scholar Michael Renov (1993, p.8) has put roughly like this: disagreement over the interpretation of a video tape resulted in a violent rebellion and damages estimated at about US$700 million.

Figure 1.13 *In 1991 Rodney King was arrested by US police. The video of his beating during the arrest was used during the subsequent court case against the police*
Source: Empics

Holliday's 81-second take shows, in unclear, badly lit pictures, that a man lies on the ground while a group of police officers stands around and above him, hitting and kicking him. This is the indexical and iconic information the images provide. The disagreement that (somewhat surprisingly to most people) arose, concerned the question of what this scene actually *meant*. Most of the roughly one billion people around the globe who saw this piece of video thought they saw an example of brutal, in policing terms, and totally unnecessary violence. One might say the overwhelming majority of television viewers spontaneously applied a moral connotational code for the interpretation of fights that awards sympathy to the underdog, a person lying on the ground while attacked by several enemies – the guy who is alone against many. But the white jury from the white suburb in the ensuing trial did not apply such a code, not after the policemen's lawyers had completed their analysis of the footage in court. Through innumerable repetitions, uses of new framings, slow-motion, reversals and stills, the video sequence was in a sense emptied of the moral and emotional significance perceived by most television viewers. The spontaneous code was replaced with another, which (finally) became possible to use. A space was opened up for moral and emotional connotational codes that members of the jury and many in their social category have readily available: black Americans in confrontations with the police are connotationally interpreted as dangerous, violent, drug-intoxicated criminals. The police officers' claim that the abuse of King was necessary because he was aggressive became believable.

8 Conclusion

Both of these very different examples show how semiotics provide concepts and ideas that may seem very abstract and far removed from actual experience and current public issues, but which become highly useful and meaningful if applied within some larger context of interpretation. We have seen in this chapter how the various tools of semiotics can help us to understand how meaning works in texts in a wide variety of ways, no matter how banal. And we have seen how processes of signifying are closely tied up with questions of textual power; for example, the power of a newspaper to ridicule health and safety regulations, or the power of television to turn a savage beating by police into a necessary technique for the control of black criminals.

Semiotics has also been hugely important in making it apparent that our knowledge values and beliefs are social rather than individual in nature. We share codes and argue about the meaning of what we see on screen, hear on the radio or read in a newspaper. Semiotic analysis can, then, help to show the means by which such meaning is made, how it is a cultural process rather than simply being a matter of the way things are.

Another way of putting this is to say that semiotics invites us to examine texts not just for their obvious content, for *what* they have to say. It also gets us to think about representation; that is, about *how* texts show us events, objects, people, ideas, emotions and everything else that can be signified. Indeed its whole emphasis is that the 'how' strongly influences the 'what'. We might therefore say that semiotic analysis is as much a frame of mind as it is a set of techniques. Crucially, it is a frame of mind which *all* the chapters in this book on textual analysis adopt to a greater or lesser extent.

DVD-ROM

Now that you have finished reading Chapter 1, work through the Semiotics activities in the Chapter Activities area of the *Analysing Media Texts* DVD-ROM. ■■■

Further reading

Bignell, J. (2002) *Media Semiotics*, Manchester, Manchester University Press. A very clear introductory text, *Media Semiotics* has a really useful focus on the media. It also has lots of illuminating worked examples.

Chandler, D. (2005) *Semiotics for Beginners*, http://www.aber.ac.uk/media/Documents/S4B/ semiotic.html. This is a terrific website. Extremely well designed and written, it is far and away the best online guide to semiotics. The glossary of terms alone is a very useful resource.

Hawkes, T. (1977) *Structuralism and Semiotics*, London, Routledge. Hawkes's classic text is a little more advanced than the two above, but it is also very clearly written; especially useful for showing the history of the ideas associated with semiotics.

References

Barnes, J. (1998) 'How was it for you?', *Time*, 20 July, pp.152–3 http://www.time.com/time/magazine/1998/int/980720/cover_story.how_was_it_f17.html (accessed 19 May, 2005).

Barthes, R. (1973) 'The face of Garbo', *Mythologies*, London, Paladin.

Barthes, R. (1977) 'Rhetoric of the image' (trans. S. Heath) in *Image, Music, Text*, London, Fontana.

Bennett, T. (2005) 'The media sensorium: cultural technologies, the senses and society' in Gillespie, M. (ed.) *Media Audiences*, Maidenhead, Open University Press/The Open University (Book 2 in this series).

Bonner, F. (2005) 'The celebrity in the text' in Evans, J. and Hesmondhalgh, D. (eds) *Understanding Media: Inside Celebrity*, Maidenhead, Open University Press/The Open University (Book 1 in this series).

Gripsrud, J. (1995) *The Dynasty Years: Hollywood, Television and Critical Media Studies*, London and New York, Routledge.

Hall, S. (1980) 'Encoding/decoding' in Hall, S., Hobson, D., Lowe, A. and Willis, P. (eds) *Culture, Media, Language*, London, Hutchinson.

Kjörup, S. (1993) 'Billedmanipulation – og den indeksikalske teori om fotografiet ('Image manipulation and the indexical theory of photography') in Gripsrud, J. (ed.) *Mediegleder (Media Pleasures)*, Oslo, Ad Notam Gyldendal.

Lodge, D. (1985) *Small World*, Harmondsworth, Penguin.

Metz, C. (1982) *The Imaginary Signifier: Psychoanalysis and the Cinema*, Bloomington, IN, Indiana University Press.

Porter, D. (1982) 'Soap time: thoughts on a commodity art form' in Newcomb, H. (ed.) *Television: The Critical View* (3rd edn), New York and Oxford, Oxford University Press

Renov, M. (1993) 'Introduction: the truth about non-fiction' in Renov, M. (ed.) *Theorizing Documentary*, New York and London, Routledge.

de Saussure, F. (1974) *Course in General Linguistics*, London, Fontana.

Schrøder, K. (1988) 'The pleasure of *Dynasty*: the weekly reconstruction of self-confidence' in Drummond, P. and Paterson, R. (eds) *Television and its Audience: International Research Perspectives*, London, British Film Institute.

Whorf, B.L. (1956) *Language, Thought and Reality*, New York, Wiley.

Woodward, K. (ed.) (1997) *Identity and Difference*, London, Sage/The Open University.

Note
This chapter is a revised version of a chapter in Jostein Gripsrud (2002) *Understanding Media Cultures*, London, Hodder Arnold.

Understanding genre

Chapter 2

Gill Branston

Contents

1   Introduction

We never engage with media in a vacuum. Rather, we enjoy and make sense of particular media texts in relation to other texts of a similar type. In media studies these types of text are known as genres (from the French for 'type' or 'kind'). They include westerns, comedy, sci-fi, horror, thrillers, soaps, news and 'reality TV'. Of course, we can classify media texts according to different criteria: by director, actor, style or some other system of categorisation. But genre is one of the principal ways in which audiences, producers and critics routinely classify media. Our cultural knowledge of media genres is woven into the very texture of our everyday lives and shapes the media choices we make, as well as the expectations and assumptions that we bring to understanding and enjoying media texts. This knowledge of media genres is acquired over many years and seems an obvious part of our common-sense understanding of the media. As a result, certain ideas we have about the way genres represent the social world become deeply embedded in our thinking.

This chapter critically examines the concept of genre, and our common-sense understandings of it. We will explore both how genre represents the world, and how it connects to intertextuality (or the ways in which texts always make reference to other texts with or without our realising). As in all branches of media studies, there are some fascinating and intensely argued debates here. When you have finished the chapter and the DVD-ROM activities, you should be familiar with these debates and, as a consequence, be able to:

■ analyse the ways in which media genres are recognised and classified by audiences, producers and critics

■ appreciate that genres are characterised by patterns of repetition as well as difference: that is, to say by 'repertoires of elements'

■ understand ways in which texts are not unique but often take hybrid forms and always relate to other texts via the process known as intertextuality

■ identify how different media genres are attributed with varying degrees of status and cultural value

■ recognise some key attributes of 'melodrama' as it operates across both factual and fictional genres.

2   Genre recognition

We mobilise our genre knowledge routinely to order our media experiences, and in doing so we come to recognise a wide range of genres. If you turn on the radio or television it is likely that, almost instantaneously, you will be able to distinguish a news programme from a comedy or dramatised serial – perhaps from the opening credits as we saw in Chapter 1. Recognising the genre of a film, a music track or a radio programme, is accomplished without much conscious thought because, as members of cultural communities, we recognise culturally specific codes and conventions that have been established over time. But in addition to being someone able to make such everyday recognitions, you are now a student of the media.

Academic approaches to media have often tried, for the sake of analysis, to categorise or isolate media products (calling them 'texts' is a prime example). Studying genre, however, means working at a 'higher' level, and dealing not only with individual texts, but with groups or families of texts. We identify patterns of similarity and difference, perhaps analysing how a text may combine elements of several genres. We look for broad patterns of change in different genres, say crime fiction or the western, and analyse what these changes reveal about political and social change, such as transformations in attitudes to crime and punishment. Popular genres can be seen as revealing underlying preoccupations and conflicts in a social order. Studying genre may reveal how the media offer mythical solutions to these preoccupations.

Genre labels (romance, science fiction, news, etc.) are used to categorise media by:

- media audiences seeking the pleasures of the familiar and the reassurance involved in knowing broadly what might happen in a particular media text;

- media industries aiming to avoid risk and ensure profitable differences;

- media critics, and others with the power to classify media, in establishing, maintaining and changing hierarchies of cultural value and status.

From the point of view of the industries, if output can be sorted into broadly familiar groups – for example, television into 'light entertainment', 'news' or 'current affairs', or films into 'thrillers' or 'romantic comedies' – then economies of scale can operate. In other words, because of the sheer scale of repetition in production, similar sets, script writers and other key players involved in the production process can be reused profitably . What is more, output can be predicted and therefore advertised, marketed and contracted in advance, and advertisers can be assured that they will have access to certain audiences. Perhaps the classic example of this is the 'Hollywood studio system' which emerged in the 1920s, when film production was dominated by a small number of integrated companies with controlling interests in the distribution and exhibition of their films. The studio system generated product standardisation and, thereby, reliable returns on investment in two ways. First, the films were characterised by a highly specific type of narrative structure (see Chapter 3 for a discussion of narrative structure). Second, genre films were developed, refined and matured into their 'classic' formulations (see Figure 2.1).

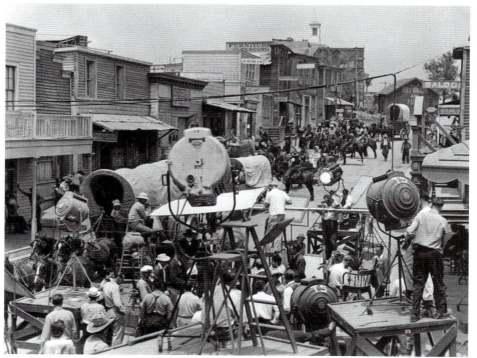

Figure 2.1 *On the set of* Cherokee Strip *(USA, dir. Selander, 1940). A classic western in the making*
Source: Ronald Grant Archive

These aspects, the standardisation and repetitiveness of genre, are vitally important. Yet in an important sense it does not tell the whole story. For, although genre films are made as part of an industrial and commercial process (and so for some people could never be considered as 'art'), they are far from simply being standardised products churned out so as to be always the same. While it is not amusing to discover that one tin of baked beans is different from the next (half empty, or full of prunes, for example), cultural products (such as films and television programmes) are sold on a blend of reassuring repetition and enlivening difference.

Many media products are publicised to us prior to our experience of them, partly through their generic features. So we know something of what to expect before we engage in the experience of watching a movie, whether on television or cinema screen. Yet despite this genre knowledge from film posters, review programmes and articles, the process and indeed the pleasure of making sense of genre products involve moment by moment recognitions, uncertainties and speculation (see Section 3 of Chapter 3 on narrative process for more about this).

To sum up, most of us have learnt to recognise the many different kinds of films, songs and television programmes that are grouped into genres. This knowledge offers the pleasure of predictability and familiarity. Yet we also expect the pleasures of difference, of being invited into interestingly unpredictable processes of guessing what happens next and of being surprised as we experience our favourite media genres. This is just like other social rituals and group routines, which play with repetition and difference across a range of elements, whether they belong to the rituals of birthday parties or funerals, greeting people or saying goodbye.

3   Genre, classification and status

As a form of classification, media genres are rather like *maps*. Different kinds of maps emphasise different features of a landscape or cityscape in order to be useful, as, for example, with road maps. Or take the classification by gardeners of plants into 'weeds' and 'useful plants' when, of course, by another system of classification, such as botany, all of these are simply 'plants'. In a famous formulation, the anthropologist Mary Douglas wrote that 'Dirt is matter out of place' (Douglas, 1966, p.163). This is part of her argument that dirt is not a natural but a cultural category, arrived at by the decision to define boundaries around what may be regarded as filthy, excremental or taboo. But, the boundaries of classification established by a particular culture, religion or society, are ritually and routinely transgressed. For Douglas, this transgression involves a creative act because it goes beyond the limits of the established classificatory boundaries and allows for the negative aspects of lived experience to be acknowledged and even affirmed. So too in media genres, genre rule breaking can be used as a creative tool for generating irony and laughter, surprise and contemplation.

The transgression of boundaries can also have horrific and repressive consequences. After the attacks on the USA on 11 September 2001, many acts of violence were classified by governments as 'terror'. The term 'terror' became a powerful generator of fear and was used to legitimate legislation that curbed civil liberties, ostensibly to assuage those fears. Such categorisation ignored the ways in which criminal and suspected criminal acts, or acts of resistance to oppressive regimes, were lumped together as having 'terrorist' motivations while actually having very different origins, histories and motives. These examples show that systems of classification are never clear cut, fixed or unchanging. Rather, they are mobilised to serve social and political goals and often have significant effects.

In the media, systems of classification have an additional function: they also establish hierarchies of values, by attributing high or low cultural status to media products. As a system of classification, genre is therefore intimately connected to power in that the attribution of low status to a media genre, say soap operas, usually involves the attribution of a similar status to the soap opera audience too. We can see, then, that studying genre helps us to understand how systems of cultural classification and taste are socially stratified, and so reflect and reinforce power relations.

Genre, as a system for classifying media products, works alongside several other, often more official, kinds of classification. Censorship and its assumptions about the appropriate age range of an audience for a particular film form one such system. Censorship expresses cultural norms about age, media use and potential media effects. Another system of classification is that established by media critics and reviewers. The terms used by reviewers acquire their own power. They are quoted on posters and other forms of advertising as well as on DVDs, for example, and work to classify our expectations and shape our judgements about media. Terms such as 'highbrow', 'middlebrow' and 'lowbrow' are also often used to both sort cultural and media products and reflect and reinforce social class structures and hierarchies of taste.

Reviews of the film *The Passion of the Christ* (USA, dir. Gibson, 2004) (see Figure 2.2) were current at the time of writing this chapter. They seemed to me to show very clearly how status and genre classifications are woven together in judging a film's worth. The film was classified as 'serious' by most critics, and as dealing in a very 'realistic' way with an important subject – the last hours in the life of Jesus Christ. The high status of the film was signified in the reviews, not only by the space and amount of attention given to its weighty subject matter, but also by the use of subtitles for the 'authentic' Roman and Aramaic dialogue (subtitles usually being associated with 'art' cinema), the sonorous music and the slow pace of much of the film. Only a few critics focused on the film's gory special effects around the crucifixion (classified by others as 'realism') and the way some spectators treated it as a test of viewing endurance or toughness.

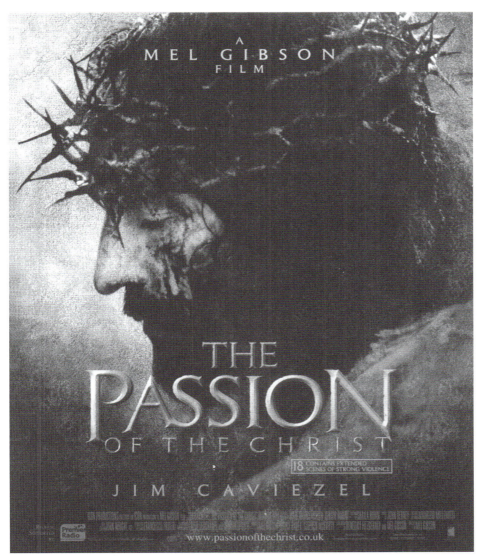

Figure 2.2 *The film poster of* The Passion of the Christ
Source: Ronald Grant Archive

The film could easily be categorised as a kind of horror film but, given the subject matter, this would be a scandalous label for some because of the low status of the horror genre and its audiences. A few critics pointed to how the film conformed to the generic convention of the 'biblical epic', which was a popular Hollywood 'mini-genre' in the 1950s. Some highlighted the suffering of Christ or the ideological connotations of the film – especially the way it played into radical religious right or conservative discourses, prevalent in the USA. Other reviews commented on the politics of representing Christ (arguably an Arab, born in Palestine) and his family by using fair-skinned actors (as in European classical paintings) rather than using more realistic looking, darker skinned actors. Yet other reviewers suggested that only certain parts of Christ's teachings are represented, certainly not those which would encourage radical social change.

Thus the reviews revealed a great deal about the ambiguous status of the film and its status as art or gory entertainment. They also highlighted the political orientations of the reviewers and their assumptions concerning what would interest readers about the film. This brief analysis points us to an alternative way of depicting the status of different cultural forms: the classifications of art and entertainment (see Table 2.1).

Table 2.1

Art	Entertainment (or 'genre' forms)
Realism	Escapism
Edification	Wish fulfilment
Serious, universal themes	'Trivial' concerns and superficial treatment
Difficult	Easy
Spiritual, intellectual response	Bodily response (as in laughing or crying)
Refined, educated audience	'Vulgar', 'dumbed-down' audience

These attributions can have material effects on the status of different media genres, on the people who work in them, and on those who enjoy their output. Clearly, they are also attributions which we, as members of the media audience, make ourselves. When, for example, was the last time you 'confessed to' a fondness for some kind of 'trash television' or low status media form? Or to put the question another way, how do you judge heavy metal music fans, or compulsive viewers of reality TV programmes, or the viewers of a television soap opera, or of a complicated science documentary? Whatever your answers they depict your relationship, as a member of a social group, to the informal rules of genre, status and pleasure.

This alignment of genre with social position and cultural value is not confined to audiences though. As we have already seen in the case of *The Passion of the Christ*, entertainment forms are often viewed by critics satisfying audiences who want nothing more than escapist fantasies or the repetition of simple conventions, and certainly not complex responses or originality. Indeed, audiences are said by some to be de-politicised or 'dumbed down' by standard genre forms. On the other hand, according to many critics, 'art' and higher status forms are characterised by difference, by claims to 'seriousness' or 'realism', or political or philosophical reflection. Yet this may simply be explained by the fact that highly educated, leisured and wealthier audiences have acquired the tastes and the cultural capital that enable them to use and make sense of high-status art forms. This in turn reflects and reinforces their high status. In circular fashion, it seems that cultural tastes and hierarchies both reflect and reinforce social hierarchies and power relations. (However, see Chapter 5 for an alternative view according to which realism, reflection and seriousness in media texts may be valuable in themselves as well as reinforcing social status.)

Perhaps the key point to take from this discussion is that no work of art or media product exists entirely outside genre boundaries. Even pre-industrial 'art' forms, whether classical music, painting, or writing, depended on shared codes, conventions and expectations. It follows that the important questions are: which social groups share which genre codes, and how are the cultural resources that give people access to these codes distributed in society?

In the end it is impossible to think of a cultural or media product that works outside genre boundaries completely. Even the most avant-garde gallery or theatre production mobilises genre expectations in one way or another. 'Scandalous' artists, like 'naughty' children, can only achieve the exciting charge of breaking the rules because we recognise the existence of these rules. Genre, and genre-breaking, it seems fair to say, is everywhere in media and culture.

4 Genres as repertoires of elements

How might we understand the blend of repetition and difference in genre forms? One way into this problem is through identifying the boundaries of genre groupings, even if these shift and are open to historical reinterpretation. For example, most of us would call *The Sopranos* (USA, HBO, 1999 to present) a television gangster series and not a soap opera (see Figure 2.3), and *EastEnders* (UK, BBC, 1985 to present) a soap and not a gangster series. Similarly, the James Bond film series, despite emphasising futuristic technology, does not currently get classified or advertised as 'science fiction' but as 'spy thriller'. Alfred Hitchcock's film *The Birds* (USA, dir. Hitchcock, 1963) was set in 'the present' and marketed as a 'thriller' (or rather a 'Hitchcock thriller', a particular sub-group), but there was no ostensible motive for the birds' horribly malevolent behaviour, and this lack might have easily pushed the film

Figure 2.3 A still from US television series,
The Sopranos

with its special effects into a 'horror' or 'supernatural' grouping. Parts of the film evoke the genre of futuristic 'eco-horror' rather than contemporary thriller, and seem to offer a warning about the impact of human behaviour on birds. The animated film *Finding Nemo* (USA, dir. Stanton, 2003) played cleverly with this kind of genre recognition through its villain seagulls and their cries of 'Me! Mine!'

Despite the existence of recognisable genre boundaries, there are only a limited number of aspects of a genre which are repeated in all the texts 'belonging' to it. They can be played and combined in a thousand ways, often with elements of other genres (see the use of horror echoes in the opening of the film *Wild Things* (USA, dir. McNaughton, 1998), for example). For a film to be successful, it requires a carefully balanced blend of repetition of and deviation from these genre elements. In fact, it is extremely difficult to identify a 'pure' genre product. We can see this even in the case of Hollywood films from the 'studio system' (*circa* 1920–1960), which nearly always contained a romantic sub-plot (regardless of whether it was a gangster, detective, horror or comedy film) to attract female as well as male audiences. The key point is that it is unhelpful to think of genres as having stable elements which simply get repeated with minor differences, or of innovation only happening when exceptional directors, musicians, etc., work in them. A more useful approach is to treat each genre as a huge 'repertoire of elements'. Any text belonging to that genre will then work by selecting and combining elements from its particular repertoire.

For cinema and television, the repertoire includes several areas:

- **Audio-visual elements**: stars, costumes, settings, camera style, lighting, editing style, music, voices and other sound effects which you would associate with particular genres. For example, some genres emphasise one type of possible camera movement from a huge spectrum: expansive pans and long shots for westerns, or in epics like *Lord of the Ring: The Fellowship of the Rings* (New Zealand/USA, dir. Jackson, 2001), frequent use of facial close ups, or carefully lit eyes for romance genres. The visual patterns of a genre are often referred to as its iconographic features: deserts and small town bars in westerns, dark gothic mansions and monsters in horror films. These iconographic elements provide us with the visual clues we need to recognise a genre. Music, speech and sound effects are also powerful auditory signifiers of genre.

- **Narrative**: most of the films we view have a classic narrative structure. This includes an opening equilibrium or state of affairs (a sort of 'once upon a time-ness') which is disrupted so that an enjoyable chain of puzzles and surprises can be set in motion, to be 'settled' into a new but different equilibrium at the end. (You will be considering this in more detail in the next chapter on narrative.) Genres develop this broad narrative structure in different ways. In many national cinematic traditions, genre 'impurity' is the norm. Bombay or 'Bollywood' films, for example, conform to a general 'formula' which mixes elements from musicals, action films and melodramas (see Figure 2.4).

  Genres can often be distinguished by the ways in which they begin and end their narratives. Western and action films usually open with an act of violence against the hero that necessitates revenge, or retaliation. The narrative then ends with an act of violence, the gunfight, where 'might' coincides beautifully with 'right' – at least, in the 'classic' years of the genre. On the other hand, the romance or 'woman's film' usually centres around a woman (rather than the conventional leading male protagonist typical of most Hollywood genres) and begins with some disruption to her personal life, often involving her meeting a man who interests her romantically, whether or not she is married. Romantic melodramas, for example, often end with the defeat of the hopes raised by this meeting.

- **Ideological relations:** genres change in relation to broad social and ideological shifts in the real social world. Genres represent the social milieux of, for example, crime, romance and espionage, in distinctive if predictable ways. One of the most important aspects of studying genre films is to analyse their ideological workings (see Chapter 5). The US Civil Rights movement of the 1950s and 1960s had a massive impact on the range of roles available to people of colour in cinema and the audiences for them. *Imitation of Life* (USA, dir. Sirk, 1959) movingly entwines the repetition of elements of a family melodrama with larger issues of racism, a narrative use of a black character 'passing' as white, and its tragic consequences (see Figure 2.5).

Figure 2.4 *The film poster for 'Bollywood' movie,* Devdas *(India, dir. Bhansali, 2002): popular Indian films combine elements from musicals, action films and melodramas*

If you think about all the possible permutations of these 'repertoires of elements', there is a lot of fluidity even in the most apparently repetitious genres. This variability is part of the mixing of genres, or 'hybridity', which has long been a feature of media output, although it is especially marked in contemporary media. Why might that be so?

5   Hybridity and intertextuality

Figure 2.5 *Sarah Jane weeps over her mother's coffin in the funeral scene at the end of* Imitation of Life
Source: *Imitation of Life*

In media-saturated cultures, the hugely varied repertoires of elements in fictional genres, already replete with potential combinations, get mixed further. These mixed genre products are often referred to in journalism and advertising as, for example, 'rom-com', 'comedy-horror' or 'noir sci-fi'. In academic discourse this genre-mixing is called hybridity, and is part of the process referred to as intertextuality (see Section 1 of this chapter). The term 'intertextuality' problematises the notion that the author is the main source, and sole creator, of the meaning of a text. It suggests that texts are tissues of meanings that draw on prior knowledge of texts. As such, texts have no clear boundaries but always refer to other texts – more or less explicitly. The choice of a title, the use of a particular phrase, object, colour or piece of music, the way the camera moves – all such elements may make reference to other texts whether self-consciously or not. Factual and fictional, print or television, all manner of texts may refer to one another (think of the celebrity gossip magazines). As viewers, we like to spot intertextual references, especially in advertisements, which often work to flatter our intelligence and make us feel media-literate. The terms 'hybridity' and 'intertextuality' are useful for thinking about how far today's dominant narrative forms in television and film (especially in Hollywood) combine genres, make references to other media texts and display self-awareness (also known as reflexivity).

Partly because of recent technological developments, the growth of marketing industries and the demands of advertising-driven media forms, what was once thought of as 'the mass audience' has been broken into many 'target 'or 'niche' groupings. Multi-channel television has, arguably, speeded up processes of fragmentation. New media products have to be found to satisfy new audiences and to some extent at least this has encouraged the development of new genres. At the same time, a recent trend in multi-channel television has been towards unsettling hybrid mixes of previously distinct genres, such as drama and documentary, or comedy and reality documentary as in *The Office* (UK, BBC, 2001–2003) (see Figure 2.6) or horror/mystery/comedy in the *Scream* film series (USA, dir. Craven, 1996, 1997, 2000). This increasing blurring of genres and modalities (that is, of fact and fiction) can make it difficult to use one's genre knowledge to identify the nature of the text. Spoof documentaries that play with conventions in order to dupe or tease gullible viewers are a good example of this.

Figure 2.6 *The David Brent character from* **The Office** *(UK, BBC, 2001–2003), giving a 'knowing look' to the audience*
Source: BBC

Many film and television texts 'wink' at the audience, in a knowing way, signalling their self-conscious playfulness with genre conventions. This reflexivity is another intertextual ploy. For example, the Austin Powers films slyly acknowledge the audience's familiarity with James Bond conventions. This flatters the audience and makes them aware of their genre knowledge. The scene involving spin-off products in the souvenir shop of *Jurassic Park* (USA, dir. Spielberg, 1993) mirrors the moment when you pass souvenirs of the film itself on sale outside the cinema. Such forms of reflexivity may disrupt the willing suspension of disbelief that realist films and television encourage in their audiences. That is, they emphasise the *artificial* nature of texts, even as they strengthen the commercial basis of film spectatorship.

Intertextual referencing is also increasingly apparent in mainstream media genres today. For example, it is sometimes used as a ploy to dramatise a news story, grab viewers' interest, and convey ideological themes. The Iraq War coverage (2003), across press and television news forms, often drew on existing repertoires of elements from Second World War fictions. It reworked themes such as 'War is hell but it makes heroes', and 'The women wait while the men fight'. It also reused the famous images of previous US 'victories', such as the photo shot by Joe Rosenthal of the planting of the US flag on the Pacific Island of Iwo Jima in 1945. (See Branston and Stafford, 2003, pp.26–9, for an analysis of the use of this repertoire of images. See Figure 2.7 for a satirical take on the Iwo Jima image.) These themes and images were previously circulated as war fictions, novels, photos, comics, paintings, poetry, statues and other kinds of commemoration, across many different wars. Such echoes of previous US 'victories' were used to signify US heroism and rally support for the legitimacy of US military action in Iraq in 2003. Using familiar templates, and instigating powerful associations in this way, can serve, and indeed challenge, powerful particular political and ideological interests.

Figure 2.7 *A cartoon created by Steve Bell signalling the dubious nature of 'victory' in war*
Source: Steve Bell

So, the idea of intertextuality challenges the idea that genres are simply repetitious and made so as to appeal to naïve audiences. However, an overemphasis on 'hybridity' or 'intertextuality' as potentially challenging or subversive of mainstream media (an argument made in some contemporary cultural comment) can ignore the ways in which not all genre texts are equally available for reference. The scales are hugely tilted towards Hollywood and mainstream cultural products. Audiences make intertextual recognitions, but often from a limited pool of resources.

All of cinema, for example, is potentially available for quotation, allusion and resonance, but it has been overwhelmingly Hollywood films and stars that have had, and still have, the most power to be 'quoted'. There are some very high-status examples of the reach of intertextuality based on Hollywood fictions. In his political speeches, US President (and ex-film actor) Ronald Reagan regularly quoted film lines such as: 'Go ahead, make my day!', which is a famous Clint Eastwood line from the film *Sudden Impact* (USA, dir. Eastwood, 1983) and 'May the Force be with you', from *Star Wars* (USA, dir. Lucas, 1977). US President George W. Bush used the tag line from countless westerns – 'Wanted dead or alive' – about his desire for the capture of Osama Bin Laden in 2001. These echoes of the western invoke not only its action and excitement, as though modern hi-tech warfare were comparable to a shoot out from the western *Gunfight at OK Corral* (USA, dir. Sturges, 1957), but they also tap into the 'good versus evil' divide of classic western narratives, and the ways in which they usually conclude with the exhilarating triumph of good over evil in a final duel or killing.

Janet Staiger (1997) explores the notion of intertextuality by focusing on the term 'hybrid'. She argues, as indeed this chapter has done, that Hollywood films have never been generically 'pure'. Media texts cannot easily be arranged into watertight categories, even if they do often repeat plot structures, character types, or iconographic conventions of mainstream media. Film producers and audiences alike seek to create order out of variety, and the process of comparing one text with another is a typical interpretative strategy among audiences. However, Staiger disputes whether Hollywood genres in the past or present are truly hybrid, at least in what she understands as the true sense of the term. Let us examine her arguments in more detail.

Reading 2.1 Activity

Now read the following extract from 'Hybrid or inbred?: the purity hypothesis and Hollywood genre history', by Janet Staiger, and answer the following questions.

- What does Staiger mean by 'hybridity' as opposed to 'in-breeding'?
- Why does she think that it is important to make this distinction?
- What kind of cultural forms are truly hybrid in her view?

- Can you think of recent media products that you would call 'hybrid' in Staiger's sense?
- Do you consider these arguments to be important for analysing film genres?

A preliminary note: by 'Fordian', Staiger means the era in Hollywood (1930s–1950s) when films were produced in a way that might be compared with a Ford automobile production-line. 'Post-Fordian', then, refers to the subsequent period (from the 1970s to the present) when film production became more 'dis-integrated', and producers and directors were more independent from the studios.

Reading 2.1

Janet Staiger, 'Hybrid or inbred?: the purity hypothesis and Hollywood genre history'

[...] I have argued that representing Fordian Hollywood films as simple examples of films that would fit into neat, coherent genre categories is an inadequate thesis both theoretically and historically. Rather, films produced during that period were perceived by producers and audiences to belong potentially to several categories. No one worried about this. Instead the lack of purity broadened the film's appeal in terms of both likely audiences who might enjoy the movie and the film's originality.

The reason, however, to expend this much effort on the problem of the purity thesis for Fordian Hollywood cinema is that the purity hypothesis is then used as the foundation upon which is built a *critical difference* for the post-Fordian Hollywood era. It is one thing to claim as Cawelti does, that genres are transforming in the early 1970s. It is another to propose that post-Fordian cinema is typified by hybridity.

The reasons for my complaint are two fold. One is that this proposed difference is just not the case. (Or both Fordian and post-Fordian cinemas are hybridity cinemas, which is not the way I want to go ...) The second reason is that the use of the term hybrid for post-Fordian cinema distorts and reduces the potential value that the theory of hybridity has for cultural scholars.

The notion of 'hybridity' comes from botany and zoology and describes the crossbreeding of separate species. (It can also apply to genera and family, so technically the term could be used for what we are discussing ...) An influential application of this organic concept to literature comes from Mikhail Bakhtin. What Bakhtin writes stresses the meeting of two different 'styles' or 'languages' derived from different cultures. He summarizes: 'The novelistic hybrid is *an artistically organized system for bringing different languages in contact with one another*, a system having as its goal the illumination of one language by means of another, the carving out of a living image of another language' (Bakhtin, 1981). Bakhtin particularly emphasizes that the event of hybridization permits *dialogue* between two languages. In botany and zoology, the function of hybridization is to produce invigorated offspring by crossbreeding, but the offspring may be sterile. So too, the hybridized literary text (often a parody) may create a strong effect, but the hybrid itself does not generate a new family.

In accord with Bakhtin's original proposition, the recognition of textual hybridity has been fruitfully appropriated by postcolonial scholars to describe the outcome of cross-cultural encounters. The editors of *The Post Colonial Studies Reader* write that an event of textual hybridity does not deny 'the traditions from which [a hybrid text] springs', nor does a hybrid event signal the disappearance of the culture from which hybridity derives (Ashcroft, Griffiths and Tiffin, 1995).

More significantly, however, a textual hybrid has effects on colonizers. Homi K. Bhabha points out that the recognition by colonizers of hybridity produced by the colonized must call into question the transparency of the colonizing authority [...] (Bhabha, 1985).

Bhabha's point here is clear: to recognize a hybrid forces the dominant culture to look back at itself and see its presumption of universality. Hybridity always opens up the discriminatory presumptions of purity, authenticity and originality from which this textual hybrid is declared to be a deviation, a bastard, a corruption. [...] In the social and communicative sense in which Bakhtin used the term *hybridity*, the notion ought to be reserved for truly cross-cultural encounters. I have to ask, are the breedings of genres occurring in Fordian and post-Fordian Hollywood truly cross-cultural? Truly one language speaking to another? I seriously doubt that the strands of patterns that intermix in Hollywood filmmaking are from different species. Rather, they are in the same language family of western culture. The breeding occurring is not cross-cultural, but perhaps, and with a full sense of the derogatory implications involved, even a *case of inbreeding.*

Moreover, Bhabha's very particular political sense of hybridity suggests that when critics encounter a cross-cultural hybrid, the questions of power, of presumptive authority, purity, and origination of the dominant genre, ought to be the focus of the analysis. Unlike Bakhtin, Bhabha stresses the historical fact of an inequality of cross- cultural contacts and communications.

I cannot, of course, do more than request that critics respect the possibility that narrowing the application of theories such as textual hybridity to a specific situation has value – both descriptive and explanatory– to scholars. However, I do make the plea. Despite all the theoretical and historical problems associated with categorizing films, perhaps the most valuable critical contribution that can be made is to analyze the social, cultural, and political implications of pattern mixing. In the above theoretical discussion none of the writers declared the project of genre criticism impossible or unworthy – only fraught with scholarly difficulties. My rejection of the hybridity thesis for the post-Fordian Hollywood cinema is not a rejection of (1) the view that pattern mixing is not occurring; or (2) the fact that post-Fordian Hollywood cinema is producing hybrids both internally within the United States and externally throughout the world economy of signs. Internal hybrids would be examples of films created by minority or subordinated groups that use genre mixing or genre parody to dialogue with or criticize the dominant. (The term *internal* implies accepting the notion of a 'nation', which is a problem for theories of post-Fordian capitalism. This is an issue impossible to take to its appropriate conclusion here.) Films by U.S. feminists, African Americans, Hispanics, independents, the avant-garde, and so forth might be good cases of internal hybrids.

Both inbreeding and hybridizing need to be studied, and genre criticism has a contribution to make towards that work. Considering the implications of how critics apply theories can help in that cultural and critical work, but distinguishing between inbreeding and hybridity throughout the history of Hollywood has scholarly potential.

References

Ashcroft, B., Griffiths, G. and Tiffin, H. (eds) (1995) *The Post-Colonial Studies Reader*, London and New York, Routledge.

Bakhtin, M. (1981/1975) *The Dialogic Imagination: Four Essays* (trans. C. Emerson and M. Holquist), Austin, TX, University of Texas Press.

Bhabha, H.K. (1985) 'Signs taken for wonders: questions of ambivalence and authority under a tree outside Delhi, May 1817', *Critical Inquiry,* vol.12, no.1, Autumn.

Cawelti, J.G. (2003) 'Chinatown and generic transformation in recent American films' in Grant, B.K. (ed.) *Film Genre Reader III,* Austin, TX, University of Texas Press.

Reading source

Staiger, 1997, pp.195–9 ■ ■ ■

Staiger argues that for a genre to be hybrid it must have a politically challenging mix of elements that, in some way, subverts mainstream cinematic conventions as well as ways of seeing and knowing the world. Truly hybrid genres, in Staiger's usage of the term, involve a mixing of two different languages: for example, those of colonisers and colonised, or of the media mainstream and of the margins. Postcolonial critics, like Homi Bhabha, analyse the hybridised cultural production of writers from formerly colonised nations (India and Africa, for example), which draw upon different national cultural streams and traditions. Postcolonial critics also analyse the writings and media created by migrant and diaspora writers and film producers (for example, the work of Salman Rushdie, Hanif Kureishi, Meera Syal, Caryl Philips, Deepa Mehta and Gurinder Chadha, among others). Creative work is not hybrid just because it is produced by those who straddle cultural divisions between different continents – it must involve a new kind of language which challenges existing power relations (see Figure 2.8).

Staiger asserts that to argue that genre transformations are apparent in Hollywood films since the 1970s is quite different to arguing that post-Fordian cinema is characterised by hybridity. However, she argues that neither of these systems of production has managed to create truly challenging hybrids. Rather, they are what she would call 'inbred' – produced from within one cultural or language system. Staiger gives no specific examples of hybrid texts but we could think about Michael Moore's film *Fahrenheit 9/11* (USA, dir. Moore, 2004). This is usually referred to as a documentary, although there has been a series of 'boundary disputes' involving reviewers who have questioned its status as a documentary and argued that it is political fiction or 'mere' propaganda. The film is a hybrid mix of investigative documentary, comedy, political rhetoric, archive footage and animation. It critiques US political culture and foreign policy and challenges the political assumptions and orientations of most mainstream Hollywood films which rarely engage directly with contemporary politics.

The Office television series, referred to earlier, with its unsettling blend of 'reality' TV and comedy, might also be considered hybrid. It combines reflexive elements, ironic distancing devices and 'fly on the wall', documentary realism. David Brent, the key character, talks to camera and often glances surreptitiously at viewers as though he is being interviewed or filmed for a documentary. But, at the same time, seemingly banal and realistic everyday office situations contain elements of hilarity that belong to sitcoms and surreal television comedies. Yet the soundtrack, unlike most sitcoms, is devoid of audience laughter – something which made it difficult to adapt successfully when it was sold in the US; television executives simply could not believe that a situation comedy would be able to attract a mass audience without the addition of 'canned laughter'.

Figure 2.8 *A still from* Bend it Like Beckham *(UK, dir. Chadha, 2002): hybrid or inbred?*
Source: Ronald Grant Archive

Clearly then, a major factor limiting cross-genre exploration is the economic organisation of the media and, in particular, the drive to maximise audiences and profitability which is built into it (see **Hesmondhalgh, 2006**).

Conversely, the film *Oración* (Cuba, dirs. Trujillo, Talavera and Rodriguez, 1984) provides an example of the kind of hybridity that can be achieved outside the capitalist market system: in Cuba film production is planned and financed by the state. *Oración* uses the life and death of Marilyn Monroe as a trigger for a political, quasi-religious commentary – a prayer – against poverty, inequality and inhumanity. It is clearly coded as a non-mainstream, alternative film and as such it may appear to operate *outside* genre conventions and dominant discourses on celebrity and politics in the form of a poem/prayer (see Figure 2.9).

a mass of heads in the darkness
beneath the beam of light

Figure 2.9 *A still from the film* Oración *in which fighter jets are superimposed on the Twentieth Century Fox logo: a truly hybrid text?*
Source: *Oración*

The text consists of a potent juxtaposition (or montage) of iconic images of celebrity alongside documentary footage of poverty, famine and violence. The film's very effectiveness and the power of its 'prayer' derive precisely from the clever cross-referencing of genres in the montage of images that slowly builds up to an explosive emotional crescendo. The emotional force released by the juxtaposition of images from genres which are normally kept apart exhorts the spectator to reject the violence of poverty and the inhumanity of violence, and to take political action. All this is 'framed' by the spoken prayer which encapsulates both the spiritual yearning and the revolutionary politics of South American liberation theology. Whatever your views on the film and its intertextual references, it is not 'inbred' in Staiger's terms. It is truly hybrid. And it is certainly not tied to advertising discourses. It is deeply emotional and political at the same time – arguably two key features of the genre of melodrama to which we now turn our attention.

Study note *You can view* Oración *in the Viewing Room area of the DVD-ROM,* Analysing Media Texts.

6 Genre, escapism, realism: a case study in melodrama

We can begin by considering one possible response to academic debates about the significance of mainstream media genres, like melodrama: 'OK, all this is interesting but isn't it basically taking too seriously, and giving too much importance to, trivia and what most people enjoy as simple escapism?' Of all genres, it is perhaps melodrama that has been subjected to the most disdain and negative academic scrutiny. As such it provides us with a good case study of popular genres and questions of realism and escapism. This section therefore looks at the much maligned but very popular genre of melodrama. This case study should help you grasp some of the complexities of debates about the status of melodrama as a genre and the ways in which it shapes even those texts which appear to be highly realistic.

Clearly, stories and entertainment are imaginary in the sense that they are made up, and do not belong to the real world beyond the studio or the writer's study. Nevertheless, all texts either subscribe to or react against conventions of realism. (We will look at debates about realism in more detail in Chapter 5). In this chapter we focus on the notion of verisimilitude (or like-life-ness). We pay money to experience popular genre texts. We spend time and imaginative energy identifying with characters, trying out different roles, thinking through various problems and working through an array of possibilities in the imaginary worlds presented to us. Melodramas, like other popular forms, can indeed be a valuable source of 'escape' from pressing everyday routines or problems. Yet in saying this there is a danger that we are suggesting that popular cultural forms are much more detached from the social world than they actually are.

In fact most of us do not watch movies to simply 'escape' or 'bliss out', as though we were taking some powerful drug or entering a dark flotation chamber. What we enjoy is the play of elements. On the one hand, these belong to the recognisably real world, whether the problems of how to conduct intimate relationships, or the perils of street fighting, or the rights and wrongs of war. On the other hand, there are elements that we savour from the media world created for us with its own rules and pleasures. These elements include genre conventions, codes for how certain characters behave, and so on. As viewers, readers and listeners we constantly commute between the real world and the media world as we 'read' a text. One of the most important ways in which we judge a text is whether it is true to life in some way or other – whether physically, socially or emotionally. But we might also ask is the film well shot? Does it have a striking narrative shape, like *Memento* (USA, dir. Nolan, 2000) or *Groundhog Day* (USA, dir. Ramis, 1993). Despite this sophisticated textual interpretation in which audiences engage, reviewers and other powerful classifiers constantly give or withhold praise and status by using such terms as 'escapist' and 'realist', as though these were quite unproblematic tags attached to particular genres. There is a need, then, to examine these terms critically.

War films provide an illuminating case study. They may not appear to be escapist due to their serious subject matter and claims to verisimilitude through the use of life-like battle enactments, accurate historical details such as generals' names, and authentic uniforms. But it is worth considering how war fictions, across a range of media, afford their audiences particular kinds of identifications and fantasies. For example, viewers can enter into fantasies of male bonding or violent aggression. Viewers may enter a space in which vicarious experiences of fear, betrayal and loathing excite and distract them. Consider for a moment the *Rambo* films starring Sylvester Stallone as the central character. As an actor Sylvester Stallone, who played the 'Rambo' character, embodies both physically and in narrative terms a kind of suffering masculinity in many of his films. This was always very different to the actor

Arnold Schwarzenegger's cinematic, and now political (he became Governor of California in 2003), image of the successful warrior (see for example, *The Terminator* film trilogy (USA, dir. Cameron, 1984; dir. Cameron, 1991; dir. Mostow, 2003)) with no pity for the defeated or the wounded. Such iconic masculine war heroes and villains most certainly provide, for some, points of identification and escape from the complications and problems of viewers' more mundane everyday worlds.

Nevertheless, war films tend to have a higher status, and are taken more seriously, than other popular genres such as melodrama. This is because they are most often valued for their supposed connection to the real. For example, the publicity around *Saving Private Ryan* (USA, dir. Spielberg, 1998) emphasised the following: the 'real' training undergone by the actors and stars; the arduous nature of the film making; the use of special effects to achieve realism; and connections to actual historical events (the late stages of the Second World War in Europe) (see Figure 2.10). However, the role of non-US forces was underplayed in order to accentuate the greatness and heroism of US forces, and thus claims to realism are undermined.

Figure 2.10 *A still from* Saving Private Ryan; *gritty realism or male melodrama?*
Source: Ronald Grant Archive

6.1 Melodrama and film

Overwhelmingly, it is the more 'feminine' genres (such as melodrama, romance and musicals) which are classified as 'escapist'. This is ironic given the emphasis in melodrama on the realities of everyday life, and intimate relationships, including bringing up children. If melodrama is an escapist genre who is escaping from what? Is the genre that, arguably, best represents women's domestic and emotional work to be considered trivial, escapist and 'soppy'? And to connect war movies and melodramas, does the circulation of aggressive fantasies in part contribute to the problems experienced by women in patriarchal societies, and explored in melodramas? These questions highlight the fact that a neat separation of 'realist' from 'escapist' genres may have much more to do with power relations in society (here the power of men over women) than the apparently realist or escapist character of the texts that are being considered.

Reading 2.2 Activity

Now read the following extract from 'Melodrama revised' by Linda Williams and answer the following questions.

- How does Linda Williams define melodrama?
- In what ways does melodrama function as a basic mode of storytelling?
- Why is melodrama thought to be a 'democratic' cultural form?
- What kinds of criticism have been levelled at melodrama as a genre by feminist critics and how have some of these been revised?

Reading 2.2

Linda Williams, 'Melodrama revised'

Melodrama is the fundamental mode of popular American moving pictures. It is not a specific genre like the western or horror film; [...] it cannot be located primarily in women's films, 'weepies' or family melodramas – though it includes them. Rather, melodrama is a peculiarly democratic and American form that seeks dramatic revelation of moral and emotional truths through a dialectic of pathos and action. It is the foundation of the classical Hollywood movie.

American melodrama originates in the well-known theatrics and spectacles of the nineteenth century stage, which many critics and historians have viewed as antithetical to cinematic realism. I will argue, however, that supposedly realistic cinematic *effects* – whether of setting, action, acting or narrative motivation – most often operate in the service of melodramatic *affects*. We should not be fooled, then, by the superficial realism of popular American movies, by the use of real city streets for chases, or by the introduction of more complex psychological motivations for victims and villains. If emotional and moral registers are sounded, if a work invites us to feel sympathy for the virtues of beset victims, if the narrative trajectory is ultimately more concerned with a retrieval and staging of innocence than with the psychological causes of motives and action, then the operative mode is melodrama. In cinema the mode of melodrama defines a broad category of moving pictures that move us to pathos for protagonists beset by forces more powerful than they and who are perceived as victims. Since the rise of American melodrama on the mid-nineteenth century stage, a relatively feminized victimhood has been identified with virtue and innocence. At least since Uncle Tom and Little Eva [in the famous anti-slavery novel, *Uncle Tom's Cabin* (Stowe, 1962/1852)], the suffering victims of popular American stage and screen have been the protagonists endowed with the most moral authority [...]

The two major strikes against melodrama were [thus] the related 'excesses' of emotional manipulativeness and association with femininity. These qualities only began to be taken seriously when excess could be deemed ironic and thus subversive of the coherence of mainstream cinema. Thus, as Gledhill notes [1987], melodrama was 'redeemed' as a genre in film studies in the early seventies through a reading of the ironic melodramatic excesses located especially in the work of Douglas Sirk. 'Through discovery of Sirk, a genre came into view' [Williams, 1984].

Sirk's gloriously overblown melodramas of the fifties – *Magnificent Obsession* (1954), *All That Heaven Allows* (1956), *Written on the Wind* (1957) and *Imitation of Life* (1959) – were enthusiastically defended by seventies film critics and theorists, along with a range of other films by Nicholas Ray, Vincente Minelli, and Elia Kazan, as scathing critiques of the family and of a repressed and perverse fifties normalcy. [...]

Critics of the fifties family melodrama delighted in the way the repressed emotions of characters seemed to be 'siphoned off' onto the vivid colors and mute gestures and general hysteria of the mise-en-scène, but they were strangely silent about the emotional reactions of audiences to all this hysteria induced by mise-en-scène [...]

As a way of surveying feminist film critics' approach-avoidance to affective responses in the study of the melodramatic women's film, I would like to summarise a debate that took place originally between E. Ann Kaplan and myself over a hypothetical female viewer's response to the melodramatic woman's film *Stella Dallas* (USA, [dir. King Vidor,] 1937). My concern here is not to reanimate old arguments, but rather to restate what, in a veiled coded way, this debate now seems really to have been about: women's attraction–repulsion to the pathos of virtuous suffering.

King Vidor's *Stella Dallas*, starring Barbara Stanwyck as the ambitious working class woman of the title whose daughter becomes her life [and who decides to give up that daughter to a wealthier family, unbeknown to her] is an excruciatingly pathetic maternal melodrama of mother–daughter possession and loss. [...]

At the pathos-filled end of the movie, the viewer sees Stella looking through a picture window at her daughter, who is marrying into an upper class milieu to which Stella herself will never belong [see Figure 2.11]. Outside the window in the rain, self-exiled from the ideal world within, Stella the mother who gives up the one thing in the world dear to her, is nevertheless triumphant in her tears. Is the female viewer so identified with Stella's triumphant tears, I asked, that she has no ability to criticize or resist the patriarchal value system that makes her presence in her daughter's newly acquired social milieu so excessive? [...]

The quintessentially feminine emotion of pathos was viewed as a key agent of women's oppression by feminists in the early and mid-eighties. Anger was viewed by feminism as a liberating emotion, pathos as enslaving.[1] [...] I wrote: 'It is a terrible underestimation of the female viewer to presume that she is wholly seduced by a naïve belief in these masochistic images ... For unlike tragedy, melodrama does not reconcile its audience to an inevitable suffering. Rather than raging against a fate that the audience has learned to accept the female hero often accepts a fate that the audience at least partially questions.'

[...]

With the great advantage of hindsight I would say that the entire *Stella Dallas* debate was over what it meant for a woman viewer to cry at the end of the film. Did the emotions swallow us up, or did we have room to think? Could we, in other words, think both with and through our bodies in our spectating capacities as witnesses to abjection? And wasn't this whole debate carried out as if men never cried at the movies? [...]

Gledhill shows, for example, how scene after scene of *Stella Dallas* permits the viewer to see a character misconstruing the meaning of an act or gesture. These scenes work, she argues, because the audience is outside a particular point of view but participating in it with a privileged knowledge of the total constellation. Pathos in the spectator is thus never merely a matter of losing oneself in 'over-identification'. It is never a matter of simply mimicking the emotions of the protagonist, but, rather, a complex negotiation between emotions and between emotion and thought.

[...] Certainly Stella, smiling through her tears, is the very embodiment of internally conflicted and complex emotions.

Figure 2.11 *A maternal melodrama which plays out the conflict between love and ambition.*
Source: *Stella Dallas*

[...]
All American melodrama is produced, and operates within, dominant patriarchal, western, capitalist discourses and ideologies. However, these discourses and ideologies are frequently contradictory and constantly in flux. Popular American movies have been popular because of their ability to seem to resolve basic contradictions at a mythic level – whether conflicts between garden and wilderness

typical of the western, or between love and ambition typical of the biopic, the family melodrama, and the gangster film[2].

The most fruitful approach to melodrama would be [...] to pick up the threads of a general study of melodrama as a broadly important cultural form inherited from nineteenth century stage, in tension with and transformed by realism and the more realistic techniques of cinema, yet best understood as melodrama, not failed tragedy or inadequate realism.

Melodrama should be viewed then not as an excess or aberration but in many ways as the typical form of American popular narrative in literature, stage, film and television. It is the best example of American culture's (often hypocritical) notion of itself as the locus of innocence and virtue [...]. What is striking in these examples [of the many sub-categories of melodrama] is the way the noun *melodrama* functions as a basic mode of storytelling. The term indicates a form of exciting sensational, and, above all, moving story that can be further differentiated by specifications of setting or milieu (such as *society melodrama*) or genre (*western melodrama*). It is this basic sense of melodrama as a modality of narrative with a high quotient of pathos and action to which we need to attend if we are to confront the most fundamental appeal of movies.

Notes

1   Later, the investigation of masochistic pleasures in looking would prove a fertile, if perhaps overly reactive, alternative to the lock-step of the sadistic-voyeuristic male-gaze paradigm. See Gaylin Studlar, *In the Realm of Pleasure: Von Sternberg, Dietrich and the Masochistic Aesthetic* (Urbana, IL, University Illinois Press, 1988); see also Kaja Silverman, ed., *Male Subjectivity at the Margins* (New York: Routledge, 1992) and Carol J. Clover, *Men, Women, and Chainsaws* (Princeton, NJ, Princeton University Press, 1902).

2   Robert Ray, for example, has noted this mythic dimension of the 'classic Hollywood cinema' citing it as one of the important elements of what Truffaut once called 'a certain tendency of the Hollywood cinema' and relating it to the tradition of Amercian exceptionalism. However, Ray may too quickly subsume this mythic, resolution-seeking nature of popular films to the subordination of style to story, of affects and effects to narrative, typical of the model of the bourgeois realist text derived from the novel. I am arguing that the 'certain tendency of the Hollywood cinema' is at least as importantly melodramatic as it is realistic. *A Certain Tendency of the Hollywood Cinema* (Princeton, NJ, Princeton University Press, 1985), 32–33, 56–57.

References

Gledhill, C. (ed.) (1987) *Home is Where the Heart is: Studies in Melodrama and the Woman's Film*, London, BFI.

Stowe, H.Beecher. (1962/1852) *Uncle Tom's Cabin; or, Life Among the Lowly*, Cambridge, MA, Belknap Press of Harvard University Press.

Williams, L. (1984) '"Something else besides a mother": Stella Dallas and the Maternal Melodrama', *Cinema Journal*, vol.24, no.1, pp.2–27.

Reading source

Williams, 1998, pp.42–88 ■ ■ ■

As you will have very likely identified, melodrama, according to Williams, is not so much a genre as a cultural mode that cuts across numerous genres. It is the fundamental form of classic Hollywood films – the popular American cultural form *par excellence* concerned with the 'retrieval and staging of innocence'. It is primarily concerned with the moral and emotional struggles of individuals who are constrained by the forces of fate, chance and circumstance. Williams claims that it is a 'peculiarly democratic and American form'. This implies that, in depicting and bringing to public awareness the everyday struggles of ordinary people, and encouraging empathy and sympathy with their plight, melodrama serves democratic purposes.

Melodramas often seem to suggest that female suffering is virtuous, noble and inevitable. The suffering heroines of melodrama appear to have greater moral authority than the other characters. (This is certainly the case with tragic heroine Annie in Sirk's *Imitation of Life*.) During the 1980s there was a lively feminist debate about the status and ideological effects of melodrama on female viewers. Some feminist critics argued that melodramas, and the tears and sadness that they induce in female viewers, serve to reinforce female oppression and collude with patriarchal domination. In Reading 4.2, Williams reconsiders this debate and revises her previous line of argument. The criticisms of melodrama were, she claims, too simplistic. Female responses to melodrama are much more contradictory and complex than the feminist debate of the 1980s believed. There is, in her view, no necessary conflict or contradiction between emotion and thought (for a discussion of viewers' responses to melodrama, see **Gillespie, 2005**). In fact all Hollywood films operate within wider ideological systems, and genre films often foreground precisely the ideological contradictions existing within a society. It is therefore useful to adopt a historical approach to the study of genre.

Study note *You can view clips from* Imitation of Life *in the Viewing Room area of the DVD-ROM,* Analysing Media Texts.

The melodramas of today have their origin in European, influenced later by American, nineteenth-century stage traditions, and still share certain continuities: the opposing moral universes of victim and villain; narrative closure in which virtue is vindicated and vice exposed; pathos and tears signalled by music and dramatic lighting, particularly of faces; and the general importance of music ('melos' in the original Greek). However, one of the reasons why the continuities between theatrical and modern media modes of melodrama are not recognised more widely is that so many Hollywood films are 'coded' in realist ways. But despite their surface realism, genres such as war films or westerns often work as 'male melodramas', allowing certain kinds of male suffering to be dramatised, imagined and explored. Many famous gangster and prison movies such as *The Shawshank Redemption* (USA, dir. Darabont, 1994) or *Angels With Dirty Faces* (USA, dir. Curtiz, 1938), or war films like *Saving Private Ryan* (USA, dir. Spielberg, 1998), work with a mix of 'gritty realism' of setting, costume, language, etc., and the immensely moving effects of melodramatic narrative shape and use of music.

Later, in her original article, Williams cites *Philadelphia* (USA, dir. Demme, 1993), *In The Name of the Father* (UK, dir. Sheridan, 1993) and *Schindler's List* (USA, dir. Spielberg, 1993) as working within the melodramatic mode. She cites two melodramatic moments in particular to illustrate her argument: in *Philadelphia*, when Tom Hanks bares his torso to the jury to reveal the marks of his skin lesions on his AIDS-stricken body; and towards the end of *Schindler's List*, when Schindler breaks down and reveals his profound regret that he did not rescue more Jews. Both moments are full of pathos, revealing the male protagonist's vulnerability and moral virtue. Both are moments when other people recognise and 'bear witness' to a suffering unleashed by a virtue (Williams, 1998, p.54).

Let us consider another example of the way in which melodrama pervades contemporary media. The life and death of Diana, Princess of Wales, is often recounted as a melodramatic story of a virtuous maiden, duped and made miserable by a powerful aristocratic husband. If you believe the melodramatic version of her life story, then the media portrayals of her death, the public's mourning and her funeral will, no doubt, have been a profoundly emotional experience for you. If, on the other hand, you believe that Diana cultivated, and was complicit with, her manufactured celebrity, and contributed to her own downfall, then you may have been a less sympathetic spectator of the media events surrounding her death. This is perhaps a good moment to consider further how certain news stories are represented as melodramatic narratives.

6.2 Melodrama and news

Melodrama and news seem, at first sight, to be very different genres. However, often they come to share basic features including a narrative emphasis on pathos and emotions. How do melodrama, an anti-realist genre according to some, and the realist genre par excellence, news, come to share similar patterns? First we must ask: in what ways can 'news' be regarded as a genre? For its producers, news has its own large budgets, specialised staff, preordained slots in radio and television schedules, and ways of being advertised. It certainly seems to be a genre in this 'production' sense. Viewers recognise its repertoire of audio-visual conventions (and object when they feel they have been broken). These include: dramatic, orchestral, 'serious' music sometimes moving to the beat of a drum (see the example of the *BBC News At Ten O'Clock*, discussed in Section 2 of Chapter 1); sets which are somewhere between an office and a science fiction control deck; a certain positioning and framing of newscasters, reporters, experts and interviewees; a 'professional' measured and unexcited voice whatever the story; 'professional' style of dress; a direct to camera/audience gaze from behind a hi-tech desk or location shot; and a narrative form which front-loads high drama and closes with a light-hearted anecdote. The final shots often show the newscasters shuffling papers and chatting which suggests that there is a return to reality, or rather a different reality to that of the news stories.

The term 'infotainment' is often used to suggest that news has strayed outside its serious, sober remit into the area of entertainment – an illegitimate hybridity for some. As well as using elements of entertainment, celebrities or film clips, often unacknowledged, in many television news stories, newspapers will often seek to make headlines more exciting by triggering genre resonances. The serial killer Frederick West's home was called 'The House of Horror' in tabloid headlines. Stories of global warming referenced *The Day After Tomorrow* (USA, dir. Emmerich, 2004), the eco-disaster blockbuster. 'Intertextuality' can signal the messiness of trying neatly to separate 'fact' from 'fiction' or entertainment. It is hard to escape the echoes and shapings of fictional forms in a world where news circulates mainly through moving images, let alone where news is subject to ratings pressures in an entertainment-filled environment. Yet these fictional shapings may angle our feelings about events in quite powerful ways, so it is important to be aware of how these processes occur.

If news is a kind of genre that represents events in the real world, melodrama involves fictionalised accounts of highly polarised struggles between vice and virtue. But these binarisms also seem to be active in celebrity news coverage or 'gossip', which often involves:

> ... a deep sense that the world is unjust, which points to a more collective sense of social inequality. To enjoy it when things go badly for 'rich and famous people' is a way of imagining cosmic (rather than political) justice taking its toll. Commiseration and indignation are equal ingredients of the pleasure of [celebrity] gossip.
>
> Hermes, 1999, p.81

Melodramatic echoes seem to have been at play in two huge 1990s news stories which transfixed the attention of US audiences. In 1994 a black motorist, Rodney King, was beaten to the ground by Los Angeles police. The beating was captured on video but the police were acquitted in a controversial trial attracting huge TV audiences. A little later O.J. Simpson, a black sports celebrity, commentator and film actor, was acquitted of the stabbing to death of his white wife, Nicole Brown Simpson. One hundred million viewers watched helicopter shots and listened to cellular phone conversations as LA police cars trailed O.J. Simpson's car. He tried to evade arrest and threatened suicide.

Linda Williams (2001) has argued that part of the power of these two very personalised news stories is the way they 'replay' two key nineteenth-century US fictional melodramatic moments. First is the best-selling novel about America at the time of slavery, *Uncle Tom's Cabin* (Stowe, 1962/1852). This novel generated white sympathy for black victims of slavery through its depiction of racial violence and its moving account of a black slave being beaten to death. Second, the big-budget, hugely popular, silent film *The Birth of a Nation* (USA, dir. Griffith, 1915) 'answered' the liberal themes of the novel with racist images of the black man as a sexual threat to white woman (which had a resonance for many US blacks who took the side of 'O.J.'). Williams (2001, p.64) argues that we need to understand the power of such fictional shapings of 'factual' news precisely in order 'to get beyond the grip of a melodramatic habit of mind'.

Another more recent, high-profile news item with powerful intertextual links and a melodramatic charge is the 'capture and rescue' of Private Jessica Lynch, who was the focus of a highly gendered tale from the 2003 invasion of Iraq (see Figure 2.12). When one US newscaster slipped into calling it the story of Jessica *Ryan*, the resonances of and similarities to a product of a fictional genre, the war film *Saving Private Ryan* (USA, dir. Spielberg, 1998), were suddenly made visible. The film had narrativised the Second World War in Europe as a US rather than Europe-centred military offensive, and as ending happily, though soberly, with the rescue of a single low-ranking male soldier. In line with classic melodramatic narrative conventions, the film allowed US virtue to triumph over vice.

Figure 2.12 *The US military briefs the media on the rescue of US soldier Jessica Lynch in Iraq. When news of her rescue broke,* Newsweek, *among other publications, used the phrase 'Saving Private Lynch' as a catchy title for their rendering of the story*
Source: Associated Press

News coverage of the Jessica Lynch story made further intertextual links to oriental and imperial adventure narratives. The item was often constructed as a tale of the 'rescue' of Jessica Lynch – a captured young, white maiden from West Virginia – from Iraq – an integral part of 'the Orient' which, in the 'western' imagination, is perceived as exotic and fascinating, but also sinister and dangerous. A wealth of echoes from American nineteenth-century frontier melodrama was also apparent in much of the news coverage – echoes such as 'capture' narratives (exemplified in *The Searchers,* USA, dir. Ford, 1956) with their exciting action sequences, and their leading figures sharply drawn as either 'virtue' or 'vice'. Finally, many of the still photo images were of a young blonde woman in modern American military uniform. This added a degree of 'realism' and 'modernity' and provided a further twist to the story. It is perhaps now easier to understand why, with the help of such familiar media templates, the 'rescue' by US Special Forces became a patriotic climax in the war on Iraq 2003.

7   Conclusion

We have come a long way in this chapter. We started by discovering how much we all know about how texts are classified and have ended up exploring ways in which news is shaped as melodrama. Along the way we have seen how genre classifications are established and reinforced through journalism and marketing. However, our appreciation of these received classifications becomes more critical, more questioning, as we slow down the swift, moment-by-moment recognitions that occur in everyday casual viewing of 'genre' products. Indeed, by using the analytical approaches adopted in this chapter we can see that genres are not at all to be taken for granted. Rather, they are constructions whose meanings may be challenged — as in the case of the war film which is at least as much a melodramatic as it is a realist text.

We have seen too how repetition is commonly understood to be the essence of genres, and the cause of the scorn poured on them. Yet, repetitiveness is also connected to the need for shared rituals, common cultural spaces and the regularity of predictable routines. And more than this, much genre output turns out to be a process involving *repetition and difference* together. Genres do not simply churn out 'stock elements' but juggle a whole repertoire of elements, and often show self-awareness when doing this.

When we think of broader ways in which media products get grouped, it becomes clear that the divisions we take for granted (between fact and fiction, entertainment and art, etc.) are not so clear cut. Indeed, some groupings remain invisible, such as the close relationship, both formal and commercial, of blockbuster movies to advertising and marketing practices.

Like any categorisation, genre labels ('a western', 'a romance') are often provisional and changeable. But they can also be used to sustain influential hierarchies of value and power. As such, if you can understand the debates around media 'genres' (and the limits of fashionable terms such as 'hybridity' and 'intertextuality') you will have grasped something fundamental about the ways in which cultures classify and value particular activities and groups of people — while under-valuing others.

Once you start appreciating that these apparently solid, 'obvious' media groupings are not so unchanging and simple, you will very likely want to challenge the hierarchies of respect and status on which they draw. You may also experience them rather differently, through enjoying their repetitions and innovations, and perhaps even by defying those prejudices which are attached both to popular genres and to their audiences.

DVD-ROM

Now that you have finished reading Chapter 2, work through the Genre activities in the Chapter Activities area of the DVD-ROM, *Analysing Media Texts*. ■■■

Further reading

Browne, N. (ed.) (1998) *Refiguring American Movie Genres*, Berkeley, CA, University of California Press.

Corrigan T. and White, P. (2004) *The Film Experience: An Introduction*, Boston, MA, and New York, Bedford St Martins.

References

Branston, G. and Stafford, R. (2003) *The Media Student's Book* (3rd edn), London and New York, Routledge.

Douglas, M. (1966) *Purity and Danger: An Analysis of the Concepts of Pollution and Taboo*, London, Routledge and Kegan Paul.

Gillespie, M. (ed.) (2005) *Media Audiences*, Maidenhead, Open University Press/ The Open University (Book 2 in this series).

Hermes, J. (1999) 'Media figures in identity construction' in Alasuutari, P. (ed.) *Re-thinking the Media Audience*, London, Sage.

Hesmondhalgh, D. (ed.) (2006) *Media Production*, Maidenhead, Open University Press/ The Open University (Book 3 in this series).

Staiger, J. (2003) 'Hybrid or inbred?: the purity hypothesis and Hollywood genre history' in Grant, B.K. (ed.) (2003) *Film Genre Reader III*, Austin, TX, University of Texas Press.

Stowe, H.Beecher (1962/1852) *Uncle Tom's Cabin; or, Life Among the Lowly*, Cambridge, MA, Belknap Press of Harvard University Press.

Williams, L. (1998) 'Melodrama revised' in Browne, N. (ed.) *Refiguring American Movie Genres*, Berkeley, CA, University of California Press.

Williams, L. (2001) 'Black and White' in *Sight and Sound*, vol.11, no.9.

Narrative analysis

Marie Gillespie

Chapter 3

Contents

1   Introduction

An Irishman goes for a job on a building site.

'Have you any work for me here?' asks the Irishman.

'Maybe,' says the Englishman, 'but you'll have to pass an intelligence test first.'

'OK!' says the Irishman. 'That'll be no problem at all!'

'Right then, can you tell me, what's the difference between a joist and a girder?'

'Ah now, let me think,' says the Irishman (pause).

'Well then?' asks the Englishman (pause).

'Oh yes!' says the Irishman. 'Sure, didn't Joyce write *Ulysses* and didn't Goethe write *Faust*!'

This joke is a narrative, and we can use it to identify three approaches to narrative analysis.

Firstly, we can examine the *narrative structure* of the joke, how it begins and ends, what happens in the middle, and what changes. We can identify the particular ways in which it combines the parts to make a meaningful whole. This kind of analysis would reveal a simple binary structure: two men, two nationalities, two jobs and, in order to cause something to happen, a verbal exchange that disrupts the symmetry. We would also look for a pattern in the development of the joke – the quest, the test and the comic punchline. We would consider what this joke shares with countless others and in what way it differs (Bordwell, 1985, p.xi).

Secondly, we can study this joke as a *process of narration*. We would analyse how information is offered, withheld or delayed and how this cues us to perform certain cognitive activities: to make inferences, to predict what might happen next. We would look at how the joke plays with our cultural assumptions, how it sets up and then flouts our expectations of jokes about Irish labourers. We would also look at the *style* of the joke: why details are regarded as unnecessary, why it is told in the present tense, how and why dialogue is used, and the timing of the punchline. Here we examine the joke as a dynamic process of communication and development.

A third way of analysing this joke as a narrative would be to examine its broader social, political or ideological meanings. This approach treats the joke as *social representation*. We can look at how this joke challenges rather than confirms ethnic stereotypes about Irish labourers in England. It defies stereotypes. We are presented with a 'labourer' who seems more familiar with the world of the great modern novelists of Ireland and

Germany than with the world of building construction. We can explore the wider history of representations of Irish people and assess what such jokes reveal about power relations between England and Ireland.

These three approaches offer insights into the ways in which narrative texts work from different vantage points: as a particular way of combining parts to make a whole, as a dynamic process of communication and meaning construction and as social representation. Although quite different, these approaches often overlap in practice and can be regarded as complementary.

This chapter concentrates mainly on the analysis of television and film narratives. It uses *Imitation of Life* (USA, dir. Sirk, 1959) to illustrate the different approaches and techniques of analysis, but you will be able to apply these to texts in a variety of genres and media forms. This introductory section explains what constitutes a narrative and why narrative analysis is valuable. Section 2 provides a set of tools that can be used to analyse the basic elements of narrative structure. Section 3 goes on to look at processes of narration, or the flow of story information: how it is delivered or withheld in ways to arouse curiosity, surprise or suspense. It also examines how visual style, cinematography and editing techniques serve very important narrative functions in film. We touch only briefly on the representational and ideological aspects of media narratives across the chapter as this is the main focus of Chapter 5. When you have finished this chapter and the DVD-ROM activities you will be able to:

- understand and analyse the basic elements of a narrative, including the difference between plot and story;

- analyse how causal, temporal and spatial relations are organised, and how these elements operate together to form a narrative;

- identify universal narrative structures and patterns of development;

- understand narration as a dynamic process: in particular how the flow of story information prompts viewers to construct the story;

- appreciate how visual style (or *mise-en-scène*), cinematography, sound and editing serve important narrative functions.

1.1 Why analyse narrative?

A narrative is 'a chain of events in cause–effect relationship occurring in time and space' (Bordwell and Thompson, 1990, p.55). All the basic elements of this definition – causality, time and space – are, as we shall see, important in narrative analysis. A narrative also *begins* and *ends*: it begins with one situation and, through a series of linked transformations, ends up with a new situation that brings about the end of the narrative. 'Narrative' is the theoretical and technical term that analysts used to refer to what, in lay terms, we usually call stories. But in narrative theory the term 'story' has, as we shall see, a very particular meaning, especially in its difference to the term 'plot'.

We can study narrative from the vantage point of the storyteller or the story receiver but a comprehensive understanding of narration requires an analysis of the relationship between the two – after all, there would be no text without both. In this chapter we study storytellers and receivers as hypothetical constructs rather than as real people. This is not to say that film directors or real audiences are not important – of course they are – but our main interest in this book is in *how* texts work, not in *who* produces them, what their intentions were or who is interpreting them and in what way.

The terms *narrative, narration* and *to narrate* have Latin roots: *narrare, narratum and narro*, derived from the term *gnarus*, meaning 'knowing' or 'wise'. These roots indicate the very intimate connection between narrative and knowledge. From our early childhood, stories are a principal source of knowledge about the world, and an important way of making sense of experience. So one reason why narrative analysis is important is because it helps us to understand how knowledge, meanings and values are reproduced and circulated in society. But media narratives do not simply reflect the real world. They provide mental schema and templates that mould our ways of perceiving, knowing and believing. Some even believe that we are born with a natural and intuitive sense of narrative and that perceiving and recounting our lives in narrative shapes is common to all human groups and societies (see **Gillespie, 2005**).

Activity 3.1

Imagine that a new friend asks you about your childhood. What do you tell them? Do you pick a string of remarkable but random, unconnected actions and events, or do you try to connect actions and events in meaningful ways? What do you do to turn your childhood into a narrative? ■■■

Everything can be narrated: the life of a nation, the conduct of war, our everyday lives, a walk at sunset, but not everything *is* narrated. Political advertising, film essays, public relations or experimental films may not contain any stories at all. Storytelling involves selecting and omitting story material. What is omitted is as important as what is selected (and not just in acts of censorship). How did you decide which bits to include and exclude? What kind of narrative did you tell about yourself? Was it a narrative about an idyllic childhood in the countryside, or a tough, rough, miserable childhood in the inner city? How did you connect events and actions?

It has probably become clear that a narrative is not a random series of events. Rather, one thing leads to another. In telling stories we try to make meaningful causal connections between events and actions. We also situate events in time and place. A narrative does not just recount events and actions, it creates them. It imposes a certain order and creates a pattern of meaning even on what might be haphazard, chaotic happenings. Understanding how media narratives work, for example, how they explain the causes and effects of events and actions, is a crucial step to understanding how media construct our knowledge of the world.

A second reason to analyse media narratives is that understanding how the social and political world is 'storied' in particular ways can help us gain insight into operations of power and, not least, the power of narrative to shape perceptions of social reality. Media narratives, like all narratives, are told from particular perspectives, privileging certain viewpoints and versions of events over others. Knowing what (and whose) stories get told or remain untold is crucial to understanding the exercise of power in society. Stories about events and characters, real or fictional, may be shaped in ways that serve the interests of powerful institutions such as government or business. Some kinds of media narratives (about war and military conflict, environmental issues or poverty), produced and circulated by large multinational media corporations, can achieve unprecedented levels of exposure, prominence and power, such that they seem to be the only version of a story to tell (see **Hesmondhalgh, 2006**).

A third reason to analyse media narratives is because they reflect and communicate continuities and change. The tale of Cinderella, for example, is known to children around the world (see Figure 3.1). It can be used to analyse changing perceptions of gender relations and roles. The earliest versions of this 'rags to riches' fairy tale date back to China in the ninth century and it did not appear in Europe until the seventeenth century (Warner, 1995). But the Cinderella of today's Disney film (passive, gullible, simple, pretty and delicate) is very different from that of previous versions of the folk tale (feisty, resourceful, intelligent, bawdy, scheming and plump). The film *Pretty Woman* (USA, dir. Marshall, 1990) is promoted as a modern version of the tale but, we might ask, what has the female protagonist done to determine her fate except be beautiful and be in the right place at the right time? In the tales recorded in earlier centuries, the Cinderellas of the past save themselves, either through enchantment or deception, intelligence or guile. Not so today in much mainstream cinema where 'happy ever after' dreams reinforce dominant values. Feminist re-tellings of Cinderella's story are harder to find in mainstream media.

Last but not least, narrative analysis is important because narratives are a key source of pleasure and satisfaction. Just think of how much time we spend telling and receiving stories of all kinds. The pleasure of stories is closely linked not only to knowledge but also to desire. In *Poetics* Aristotle (384–322 BCE) argued that stories give us pleasure through their 'imitation of life' or their mimetic qualities, as well as through the movement and rhythm of their telling – through their surprising twists and turns

Figure 3.1 *The* Cinderella *story has been reproduced for centuries all over the world: (top left) a nineteenth-century drawing by Albert Hendschel; (bottom) Leslie Caron as Cinderella in the film* The Glass Slipper *(USA, dir. Walters, 1955); (top right) Richard Gere and Julia Roberts in the film* Pretty Woman *(USA, dir. Marshall, 1990)*
Source: (top left) akg Images London, (bottom) and (top right) Ronald Grant Archive

(Aristotle, 1996). Stories engage us in emotional, intellectual, visceral, moral and spiritual ways – how else could we explain our unquenchable appetite for them? Stories are about not only the desires of characters but also our desires as audiences. They invite our identification. Stories are nearly always about the projects or goals of individuals or groups, the obstacles they face, and the detours they must take to achieve their ambitions and desires. Our engagement as audiences in the *process of narration* is itself driven by desire in the form of *epistemophilia*, or the desire to know: to discover secrets, to uncover lies, to know what happens next, to see how things will end – in the satisfaction of the desire to know (see Figure 3.2). There is narrative pleasure too in the delayed fulfilment of desire. We also take aesthetic pleasure in the form and shape of a narrative: in its patterns of development, similarities and differences and, as Aristotle expressed it, in the unities of time, place and action (Aristotle, 1920 translation). How else can we explain the complete rapture, the enchantment, the suspension of disbelief, the total immersion in the story world, the consolations and discomforts that stories can generate? How can we explain or begin to analyse their value?

Figure 3.2 *The enchantment of stories crosses all social and cultural boundaries but how do storytellers captivate audiences?*
Source: Corbis

Stories are a universal phenomenon and they may even share universal structures. But does the fact that stories are everywhere and are therefore commonplace suggest they are not worth studying? Roland Barthes, the French semiotician, argues that the study of narrative is one of the most important areas of human enquiry.

Reading 3.1 Activity

Read the following extract from Roland Barthes, 'Introduction to the structural analysis of narratives'. As you read, think about the following question: according to Barthes, what are the common features of narrative and why are they valuable?

Reading 3.1

Roland Barthes, 'Introduction to the structural analysis of narratives'

The narratives of the world are numberless. Narrative is first and foremost a prodigious variety of genres, themselves distributed amongst different substances – as though any material were fit to receive man's [sic] stories. Able to be carried by articulated language, spoken or written, fixed or moving images, gestures, and the ordered mixture of all of these substances; narrative is present in myth, legend, fable, tale, novella, epic, history, tragedy, drama, comedy, mime, painting (think of Carpaccio's *Saint Ursula* [see Figure 3.3]), stained glass windows, cinema, comics, news items, conversation. Moreover, under this almost infinite variety of forms, narrative is present in every age, in every place, in every society; it begins with the very history of mankind and there nowhere is nor has been a people without narrative. All classes, all human groups, have their narratives, enjoyment of which is very often shared by men with different, even opposing, cultural backgrounds. (It must be remembered that this is not the case with either poetry or the essay, both of which are dependent on the cultural level of their consumers). Caring nothing for the division between good and bad literature, narrative is international, trans-historical, trans-cultural: it is simply there, like life itself.

Must we conclude from this universality that narratives are insignificant? Is it so general that we have nothing to say about it except for the modest description of a few highly individualised varieties, something literary history occasionally undertakes? But then how are we to master even these varieties, how are we to justify our right to differentiate and identify them? How is novel to be set against novella, tale against myth, drama against tragedy (as has been done a thousand times) without reference to a common model? Such a model is implied by every proposition relating to the most individual, the most historical of narrative forms. It is thus legitimate that, far from the abandoning of any idea of dealing with narrative on the grounds of its universality, there should have been (from Aristotle on) a periodic interest in narrative form [...]. Keeping simply to modern times, the Russian Formalists, Propp and Lèvi-Strauss have taught us to recognise the following dilemma: either a narrative is a rambling collection of events, in which case nothing can be said about it other than by referring back to the storyteller's (or author's) art, talent or genius – all mythical forms of chance – or else it shares with other narratives a common structure which is open to analysis, no matter how much patience its formulation requires. There is a world of difference between the most complex randomness and the most elementary combinatory scheme, and it is impossible to combine (to produce) a narrative without reference to an implicit system of units and rules.

Reading source

Barthes, 1997/1966, pp.79–81 ■ ■ ■

Figure 3.3 The Dream of St Ursula, *by Vittore Carpaccio (1495). This is the fifth in a sequence of nine famous paintings that recount the life of St Ursula: a popular saint and an icon of female virtue and self-sacrifice whose life was narrated in many forms across centuries. The final image shows how her brave defence of the Christian faith led to her martyrdom; Ursula's Dream is thus a premonition of her future death*
Source: Galleria dell' Accademia, Venice

Barthes draws our attention, eloquently, to the translatability and ubiquity of narratives in our lives. Narrative is a fundamental cultural form across time and across cultures. The same narrative may take many different forms, appear in myriad 'substances' and genres. He suggests that, despite their multitudinous expressions, we can identify underlying narrative structures and conventions and that these are worthy of analysis. So let us now move on and do just that.

2   Narrative structure: plot and story

One of the fundamental distinctions made by many narratologists (or analysts of narrative) is between story and plot (sometimes called story and 'discourse': cf. Chatman, 1978), and it is basic to any understanding of narrative. We shall look at this distinction a bit more closely as it helps us understand not only how a narrative is put together and how it works, but also how we make sense of it.

Let us start with the term 'story' and its very particular meaning in narrative theory. Part of the pleasure of watching a film is that we make inferences about actions and events based on the story information that we are given. For example, in the opening scenes of the film *Imitation of Life* (USA, dir. Sirk, 1959) we are given various clues: we see a crowded beach, we hear fairground music and we infer that it is summer and holiday time. Then we observe Lora (Lana Turner) moving frantically and calling out 'Susie! Susie!' We infer that she is looking for someone (see Figure 3.4). Could it be her daughter? We have dropped into the middle of a (fun?) day out at the beach and a problem. Soon our guess is confirmed. Lora has lost her little girl, Susie. We cut then to a scene of a woman, Annie, with two little girls and immediately we infer that one of these is Susie. This is also confirmed a moment later. We assume that Annie has found Susie, though we do not see her find her.

Study note *You can view clips from* Imitation of Life *in both the Semiotics section of the Chapter Activities area and in the Viewing Room of the DVD-ROM,* Analysing Media Texts.

Throughout the course of a film we make assumptions and inferences – about characters, the causes of their actions and events, the sequence and timing of events and where they happen, which may never actually be presented to us. We may not even be aware that we are doing so. Some inferences are more or less immediately confirmed or denied; others endure throughout the story and we may never find out if we were right or wrong. So a story is not just what we see and hear. It is the sum total of all the events that are presented to us explicitly, as well as those that we infer (Bordwell and Thompson, 1990, p.56). The entire 'world' in which the action takes place is often referred to as the diegesis (meaning 'recounted story' in Greek).

Figure 3.4 *The opening scenes of* Imitation of Life *invite us to infer several things about the characters, their motivations and the order and timing of events*
Source: *Imitation of Life*

In *Imitation of Life*, the people, the beach and the promenade that we see and/or hear are diegetic – but so are all the people and places that we do not see or hear (the non-diegetic elements). They, too, are a part of the world that the film represents.

The term 'plot' refers to everything directly presented to us and the order in which it is presented. In a film it is what we see and hear. In *Imitation of Life* we see two events: Lora looking for Susie and Lora finding Susie. The film's plot may also include additional material: the film starts with opening credits to the theme tune/song as the screen fills up with diamonds in slow motion. These elements are from outside the world of the film (the characters cannot see the diamonds or hear the song). So the plot of a film, the entire film, incorporates diegetic and non-diegetic material.

The relationship between story and plot is shown in Figure 3.5. Notice how they overlap in respect of explicitly presented events. Notice too how they diverge. The story extends to include all the events that we infer. The plot goes beyond the story to include what we witness directly as well additional material from outside the diegetic world.

Figure 3.5 *The relationship between story and plot overlaps in terms of explicitly presented events. Plot, however, includes elements that are not directly witnessed and are, therefore, non-diegetic*
Source: Bordwell and Thompson, 1990, p.57

As David Bordwell and Kristin Thompson point out (1990, p.57), the film-maker in a sense turns the story into a plot while we the viewers turn the plot into a story. The storyteller chooses what story information to present and to omit. The story receiver pieces together the information presented as well as hinted at and creates the story in her or his imagination. So, too, when we tell a friend about the latest film we have seen we might summarise the plot (that is, start with the first thing we actually saw and then work our way through the main events as they occurred on screen to the end), or we might offer a summary of the story (that is, tell the first event that the plot led us to infer and proceed until the end). In re-telling the story of *Imitation of Life* we might begin with the death of Lora's husband and her departure for New York to fulfil (his and) her wish for her to become an actress. Since it is a double narrative about two women, our re-telling would also include Annie's forced departure from the South due to the racism that she and her daughter Sarah Jane experienced. Neither of these events are presented to us directly of course, but they are crucial – they motivate the narrative.

So to summarise, a narrative is a sequence of events that are linked causally in time and space. The distinction between plot and story shows us what storytellers do to form a narrative and what we do as story receivers to make sense of a narrative, and how these two elements interact, overlap and differ. The definition and the story/plot distinction provide a set of basic tools for narrative analysis. The story/plot distinction is also important, as we shall see, to understanding all three dimensions of narrative: causality, time and space. Let us now consider what causes things to happen in a narrative and how actions and event are linked in time and space.

2.1 Causality, time and space

The plots of conventional feature films usually present events, as well as their causes and effects, quite explicitly in order to hook us into the narrative and give us a reasonable basis on which to infer and predict what might happen next. But there has to be some openness in the causal logic of the narrative. We should not be able to guess too easily what will happen next, otherwise there would be no suspense, curiosity or surprise.

Causality

In conventional Hollywood films, characters and their particular traits (attitudes, beliefs, values, talents, tastes, appearances, psychological dispositions, past experiences) are usually the main agents of change. They are usually the cause of events in a narrative. It is useful to analyse the different ways in which characters motivate a chain of events, though accidents, natural disasters or supernatural intervention may also function to motivate events and actions. If a film or television programme is based on narrative logic, then one camera shot leads to another in a cause–effect chain. For example, if we see a woman pointing a gun in shot A and a man falling to the ground in shot B, then we infer that the event in shot A caused the event in shot B – that is, she shot him! If we reverse the shot order, the causal link is broken and the logic of the two shots becomes incomprehensible. Scenes, as well as individual shots, are linked in cause–effect chains.

Mainstream film and television narrative usually has a 'tight' cause–effect logic so that the viewer can see clearly how one scene relates to the next. We can see this by analysing a little more closely the first three scenes of *Imitation of Life*. The cause–effect logic in these three scenes is very tightly structured. In the first scene, at the beach, Susie is lost and found and this event creates a chance meeting which brings together all of the five main characters of the film (see Figure 3.6). Two narrative problems are identified in the first scene: Annie's homelessness and Lora's need of domestic and childcare support. Both are resolved in scene three. A further two narrative problems are set up in the second scene: Sarah Jane's deep awareness of racism and her negative feelings about being black, and Lora's overwhelming desire for stardom.

Activity 3.2

Imagine these scenes (or indeed the opening scenes of any television programme or film) taking place in reverse order. It might be plausible but would it be logical? It might create a mystery but would it make any sense? ■ ■ ■

Figure 3.6 *The opening scenes of* Imitation of Life *are carefully crafted to introduce all five of the main characters and initiate the narrative 'problems' that will be resolved during the course of the story. In so doing, they set up a tightly structured cause–effect logic* Source: *Imitation of Life*

Analysing the opening scenes of a narrative is usually revealing. In *Imitation of life* they set up the double narratives of racism and celebrity with remarkable economy. Of course, the plot can present story material in many different ways, but the opening scenes of conventional plots usually only present information that is relevant to setting up the narrative situation, introducing significant characters and making enough causal connections to hook the viewer in.

Of course, plots withhold and delay important information too, leading us to make multiple inferences and predictions about causes and effects. Take the classic detective story. The plot does not usually present the causes of events or the order in which they occurred: how a crime was (1) conceived; (2) planned and (3) committed. Instead it usually presents the effects of actions in the following order: (4) the discovery of the crime; (5) the investigation by the detective; and only later (6) the revelation of (1), (2) and (3). We gradually piece together the story (1–6) from the plot (4–6). So a sense of mystery is created by withholding important story information. Information about causes (1–3) is withheld by the plot which only presents effects (4–6). Alternatively, plots may present causes (1–3) but not effects (4–6), which triggers our imagination and encourages, often intense, speculation. The story/plot distinction is important not only to our understanding of narrative cause and effect, but also to our understanding of narrative time.

Time

In analysing narrative we need to examine how time is structured and represented. In time-based media texts (film, television and radio) a key distinction is made between *plot time* and *story time*. Story time is the time period that the whole story encapsulates. In *Imitation of Life* the story time stretches back to Lora's first marriage and to Annie's life in the South. The plot time encapsulates about 12 years in the lives of the characters (1946–1958). Another kind of time to consider is *screen time*, or the time it takes to watch a film or a television programme.

The multiple, interwoven narratives in drama *serials* or soap operas may be split over weeks, months and, even, years. Soaps appear to take place in *real time* and to parallel the time of our own lives. An episode may take half an hour to watch but the plot usually covers the events taking place during the course of one day. By contrast, the narratives of television *series* (for example, sitcoms and police series) are usually contained within one episode. With each episode we return to a familiar narrative problem, albeit played out differently, and to a seemingly continuing present.

Narratives organise and represent time in different ways, and it is important to analyse how they do so. We can identify three types of time relationship in film and television texts – *order*, *duration* and *frequency*.

The *order* of events can shape, in quite powerful ways, the build up of dramatic tension, the climax and the closure of a narrative. This was apparent in the example of the conventional detective plot mentioned above. Most mainstream visual narratives follow a linear, chronological order. Even so, there are exceptions: two re-ordering devices in particular are commonly used. A *flashback*, such as in *Citizen Kane* (USA, dir. Welles, 1941), moves from present to past so that events A, B, C, D can be related in the order B, C, A, D, with A being the flashback. When faced with a flashback we infer the order of story events from the plot and we rearrange events chronologically in our imagination. A *flash forward* moves from present to future and is not so common (although the preview or trailer might be considered to be a kind of flash forward). A good example of the use of flash forwards to indicate premonitions can be observed in the chilling psychic thriller *Don't Look Now* (Italy/UK, dir. Roeg, 1973).

The *duration* of events is the relationship between the time taken for the events to occur in the plot and the time taken for them to occur in the story. In *Imitation of Life* the period of Lora's rising success as an actress from 1948 to 1953 is summarised in a *montage* sequence in which we see a rapid succession of shots of Lora on stage, exterior shots of theatres, titles of productions and adoring audiences. This *montage* sequence compresses and summarises a passage of time and uses film techniques that distinguish it from other segments. For example, the soundtrack of applause for Lora provides a sense of continuity over a very discontinuous set of images. Inter-titles, or bits of text cut into the film to signify the passage of years, are also used.

Study note *You will find a clip of this montage sequence from* Imitation of Life *in the Viewing Room area on the DVD-ROM, Analysing Media Texts (clip 4).*

The term *montage* is often used as a synonym for editing, as well as to refer to the particular approach to editing developed by Soviet film-makers in the 1920s (see Figure 3.7). It emphasises the discontinuous relationships between shots. Montage juxtaposes images in such a way as to create often powerful political meanings that are not present in the images themselves; as for example in *Oración* (Cuba, dirs. Trujillo, Talavera and Rodriguez, 1984), clips of which you can see on the DVD-ROM, *Analysing Media Texts*.

Plot duration selects from story duration and presents significant stretches of time over several days, months or years. *Imitation of Life* has a screen duration of one hour and 55 minutes, a plot duration of 12 years (events from the period 1946–1958 are presented) and a story duration of about 18–20 years (inferred events date back to Lora and Annie becoming mothers).

Editing, or the techniques used to regulate the relationship between camera shots, moves the story forward, cutting the passage of time between actions and events when it is important dramatically that the viewer should not know what happens next or when events become irrelevant to the narrative (for example, going to the toilet, or sleeping). The omission of intervals of both story and plot duration in the *viewing time* is known as *ellipsis* or *elliptical editing*. Ellipsis also refers to the shortening of plot duration by omitting intervals of story duration (Bordwell and Thompson, 1990, p.409).

The editing or stitching together of individual shots controls the timing and pace of the narrative. This is a powerful tool which can slow down or speed up the pace and rhythm of the narrative. Editing can help create suspense, curiosity or surprise. Television advertisements and pop music videos have a very fast-paced editing. 'Fly on the wall' documentaries, in contrast, may have very few cuts and present the action in long stretches of *real time*. Conventional film and television narratives use the techniques of 'continuity editing' to stitch shots together to create an apparently invisible, seamless flow, give the impression of a continuity of time and space, and knit the spectator into the narrative (sometimes called 'suture').

The *frequency* with which any one event is presented by the plot is another feature to look out for. The same event may occur several times but if a film uses multiple narrators this event will be recounted from a different character's perspective, as in *Pulp Fiction* (USA, dir. Tarantino, 1994) or recounted by a different character in flashback, as in *Citizen Kane*. Through such devices we may be provided with new information, or understand an event or a character, or the causal connections between them, in a different way.

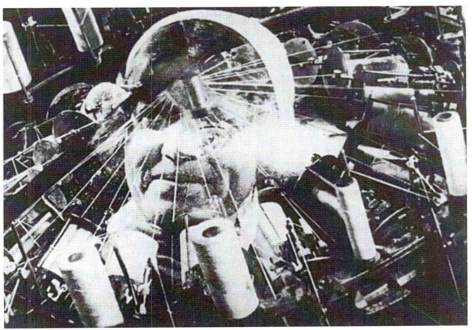

Figure 3.7 Man with a Movie Camera *(Soviet Union, dir. Vertov, 1929). Montage techniques were widely used by early Russian film makers to make powerful political statements about the exploitation of workers. Vertov was a prime exponent of montage techniques*

Space

Some media tend to emphasise time or causality but the creation of narrative space is also very important. So too is the movement of objects and figures within that space. Everything from turning to look at someone, or a gentle gesture, to the crashing of a car, or the sinking of a ship, can have narrative significance, as in, for example, the film *Titanic* (USA, dir. Cameron, 1997). The movement of figures and objects contributes to the onward thrust of the narrative. They help instigate the cause–effect chain of narrative movement. All narratives occur in some setting or social space and all narratives consist in a dynamic movement across space.

We can distinguish between plot space and story space. Plots present places explicitly (plot space) or can lead us to imagine places that we never actually see (story space), as in where Annie and Lora lived before moving to New York. We get to know the spatial world of the film or television programme through the plot space and setting. We shall examine how narrative space is constructed in more detail in Section 3, when we discuss *mise-en-scène*, because this is one of the most important ways in which narrative space is communicated and attributed with narrative significance. For the moment, suffice it to say that this French term literally means 'putting on to a stage', or the staging of events for the camera by director, producer, scriptwriter, cinematographer and others. It refers to all the elements placed in front of the camera to be filmed: the settings and props, lighting, costumes and make-up, and figure movement and behaviour or acting.

To summarise, in analysing the structure of any media narrative we need to think about the following:

- the cause and effect logic that connects events;
- the characters and how they motivate events;
- the temporal order, duration and frequency of events, as well as how time itself is represented;
- how the plot manipulates and communicates spatial information, and how narrative space and movement in space is constructed and made meaningful.

Causality, time and space structure narratives in any medium, but what, if anything, do narratives share regardless of the medium in which they are communicated?

2.2 Universal models of narrative development?

Aristotle, in *Poetics*, made the simple but profound remark that a good story must have a beginning, a middle and an end. All narratives have a basic structure and this simple three-part structure is the way in which stories are commonly discussed. But do all narratives, whether in the form of a novel, a sitcom, a radio drama or a feature film, share the same or similar patterns of development? Some theorists think so, and have sought to uncover universal narrative structures. In this section we are going to look at universal models of narrative structure and development and see how far they can be applied to contemporary media narratives.

The Bulgarian narratologist Tzvetan Todorov argued that a narrative operates as a system with its own internal logic or grammar. Most narratives, he argued, are motivated by a force or power that creates a problem or a disturbance in an existing state of affairs. The movement from the original, relatively stable, situation to another but different stable situation is punctuated by a series of disturbances, complications and obstacles. He argued that all stories follow this core narrative pattern (Todorov, 1977/1971). In other words, a narrative consists of a transition from one equilibrium, via a dis-equilibrium, to a new, revised equilibrium. This is a way of schematising the sequence which forms the typical meaningful whole of a narrative. Not all the moments in this narrative structure are presented by the plot, but as readers we infer them. An adapted and expanded schema based on Todorov's ideas follows:

1 *Exposition* – the initial equilibrium, a state of normality, stability, social order.

2 *Disruption* – a causal event by an agent of change creates a dis-equilibrium, upsetting the initial state of affairs, creating a lack, a problem or a quest.

3 *Complication* – a series of obstacles occur, which continues the state of dis-equilibrium.

4 *Climax* – dramatic highpoint of conflict, excitement or tension, followed by release.

5 *Resolution and closure* – main protagonist resolves the problem, obtains goal, fulfils desire or lack, restores order and instigates a revised equilibrium as the story ends.

The transitions from one stage to the next, the turning points of the narrative, involve crucial events which change the course of the narrative action. Characters and situations are transformed in the process of disruption. The disruption enables characters to transgress their 'normal' behaviour. This is often called the 'liminal' phase – meaning that behaviour is at the threshold of normality, order and stability. In the final stage, characters, actions and behaviour are 'normalised' and returned to a revised state of affairs or equilibrium.

Let us see if Todorov's model applies to *Imitation of Life*:

1 *Exposition* – two single women, one black and one white, struggling to bring up their daughters and achieve their goals, meet on a beach and decide to help each other out.

2 *Disruption* – their chance meeting ends in the formation of a new all-female household with Steve as onlooker/helper/romantic male hero. How will their relationships (domestic and romantic) work out as they each seek their own (conflicting) visions of love and happiness?

3 *Complication* – Lora is successful but emotionally detached. 'Something is missing', she complains. Susie falls in love with Steve who loves Lora. Sarah Jane rejects her mother Annie, denies her true identity and runs away. Annie, broken-hearted, falls ill.

4 *Climax* – Annie dies. In the spectacular funeral scene Annie's life is celebrated by the crowds who mourn her, and by a powerful solo of *Trouble of the World*, a black spiritual song. Sarah Jane arrives at her mother's funeral too late to tell her that she really did love her.

5 *Resolution and closure* – Lora takes Sarah Jane and Susie in her arms and they depart in the funeral car. The final shots show the three women in a tight embrace with Steve as an onlooker. Arguably, a new loving family unit has been created.

The model is so general that it can apply to almost any conventional narrative, although each stage of narrative development can be studied in greater detail in any medium. The exposition introduces us to a state of normality or a stable situation. The disruption creates the dis-equilibrium and sets out the narrative problem or enigma and establishes character traits and motivation. The main bulk of any narrative consists in the complication phase in which a causal chain of action–reaction is played out. The narrative problems or enigma is solved and a revised state of affairs comes into being.

One important step in analysing narrative structure is to compare the initial and final equilibrium. In *Imitation of Life* the initial equilibrium involves two sets of single mothers and their daughters. The final equilibrium reconfigures the family set-up, symbolically annihilates the troublesome (for Sarah Jane) black mother, and 'restores' an (imitation of) an all-white nuclear family consisting of Steve and Lora, Susie and Sarah Jane. The analysis of narrative structure thus leads us to an interpretation of the implicit ideological meaning of the closure – the symbolic restoration of a white nuclear family. Whether the huge black audience that turned out to see this film in 1959 would have 'read' the film in this way is, of course, another matter (see Chapter 5).

Another important step in narrative analysis is to examine in detail the precise nature of the initial disruption – the way in which the plot is triggered and motivated as a process. The nature of the disruption can be generic. In westerns, for example, the disruption is usually caused by an intruder or an invasion from outside the community, or a quest for a person or object. A news story enacts a disruption or upset to the putatively 'normal' state of affairs prior to switching the television on. In a horror story the disruption is caused by a monster.

A key type of narrative is based on a quest structure. The Russian folklorist Vladimir Propp, one of the most influential narratologists, studied a hundred Russian 'wonder tales' (see Figure 3.8) (Propp, 1968/1928). He sought a reliable way of organising and categorising them. He found that all of these narratives were constructed as a fixed sequence of exactly 31 actions (Propp, 1968/1928, p.21). Propp described these actions as functions of the hero's journey.

Propp identified a limited number of roles or functions performed by characters in the wonder tales, but he avoided defining characters in terms of individual psychology and, instead, defined them in terms of their narrative function. He identified seven roles. These could be carried out by a smaller number of characters, or one character might even perform several roles. The roles he identified are:

1   the villain
2   the hero/chief protagonist and main agent of narrative change
3   the donor who provides the hero with a magical gift
4   the helper
5   the princess and her father (or the sought-for persons)
6   the dispatcher who sends the hero on his way
7   the false hero.

Figure 3.8 *An illustration for a Russian folk tale,* Prince Ivan and the Grey Wolf. *A nineteenth-century engraving after a watercolour by Zvorikine*
Source: The Art Archive

The folk tales, he argued, were all based on the same formula. The 31 functions include:

■   initial situation
■   injury to victim or lack of an important object
■   hero's journey quest
■   donor (toad, hag-bearded man) or magical agent (ring, horse, lion), who helps

- villain or opponents, struggle, conflict and/or combat
- tests
- victory
- return, involving retardation, further obstacles or possible intrusion of a false hero
- reward, marriage, or the coronation of the hero.

The quest or hero's journey structure is used in many documentaries as well as Hollywood movies and you may be surprised at how easy it is to apply it to a range of media texts. For example, in *Imitation of Life* all five characters have a quest object – love – but all are in pursuit of different aspects of love (fame, recognition, acceptance, security, respect), some of which, the film shows, are false. Quests always involve problems and conflicts (racism, sexism, shame, insecurity, disavowal). The subjects of the narrative have helpers and opponents who push the narrative forward and hold it back at the same time, creating dramatic tension. Eventually, via a process of communication, the helpers or donors deliver the object of desire to recipients. The simplicity of this bare structure unlocks some of the complexities of narrative meanings.

Todorov's and Propp's models can be applied to all kinds of texts – advertisements, crime series, situation comedies, etc., and it is instructive to analyse not only fictional drama but also news and documentaries in this way. News and documentaries are often based on the hero's journey or quest structure. The narrator (as hero) sets out on a journey to uncover a mystery or find a treasure, meets with obstacles and opponents that prevent him or her discovering the 'truth' of a situation, but finally, with helpers, there is a transformation of knowledge, a return and a reward.

Travel, cookery and property make-over series often follow the quest narrative structure. Take a Jamie Oliver cookery programme – it involves Jamie Oliver in a 'journey' to find a real or symbolic object (say, good quality, organic local food produce); a cause–effect logic (a sequence of culinary steps); a helper (a friend calls round); magic ingredients (spices); a romance with obstacles (he has a wife to attend to as he spends so much time cooking); a reward and a happy ending (enjoying dinner with a group of friends). With property make-over programmes, the villain often comes in the shape of the plumber or the builder and much of the programme may be about overcoming problems, trials and tests.

It is well worth seeing how far you can apply Todorov's and Propp's models of narrative development to a range of media narratives. However, it is questionable whether their models are applicable to any text. Media texts today are not all quite so 'black and white' as are Russian fairy tales or the *Decameron* (a compendium of Renaissance stories by Boccaccio), on which Propp's and Todorov's models are based. These models are not very sensitive to moral ambiguity, nor do they easily elicit social and political critique or capture the complexities of meaning. They are also reductive in that we tend to lose sight of the specificities of an individual text. They are, in sum, more concerned with *how* texts mean than with *what* they mean. So, the latest episode of a soap opera becomes indistinguishable from a film by the Russian film-maker Tarkovsky.

Nevertheless, it can be fascinating and instructive to draw parallels between the narrative structures and patterns of development of Hollywood films, Shakespeare's plays and tabloid news stories. The models allow us to see a narrative grammar at play and to understand basic plot types. They may also enable us to see how the texts of a particular time, place or director belong to a basic plot type (see, for example, the *Star Wars* trilogy or the Harry Potter series of children's novels), which is then modified and altered until it exhausts itself.

The analysis of narrative structures and patterns of development is essentially a static approach. Even when we look at the transformations that take place in the movement between two equilibriums, we still have to treat the text as if it were a static structure. So to complement this approach, we need to study narrative as a dynamic process of movement and communication, the flow of story information and viewer's activity.

3 Processes of narration: the viewer's activity

In oral storytelling we can easily identify a narrator, but with film and television, where collaborative production is the norm, it is difficult to identify precisely who or what narrates. Is the narrator a creative worker (a script-writer or, like Douglas Sirk, a director) or an artistic technology or technique (the camera, the editing, the *mise-en-scène*)? Is the narrator in the text overt (someone placed in the story world) or covert (situated outside the story world and not obviously present), or does the narrator seem to be absent (as in the case of many realist texts which appear to flow naturally, masking the artifice of their telling) (see Chatman, 1978, p.146)?

Bordwell (1985) argues that when we watch a classic narrative film we see events unfold before our eyes without the impression that someone is telling us a story. He argues that it is we, the viewers, who effectively construct the story out of what we hear and see. This approach to narration or the flow of story information emphasises the active nature of viewing and provides a useful way of analysing the viewer's activity.

In this next section, we examine key features of film narration and style in *Imitation of Life*. The aim is to show how narration pulls us into a process of story construction. In particular we look at two of the most important aspects of narration: range and depth of knowledge. Then we examine more closely the use of *mise-en-scène* because, alongside editing, it is another of the most significant ways in which relevant knowledge is communicated in the film.

The essential aim of viewing activities, according to Bordwell, is the construction of a meaningful story from the plot. Viewing involves us in a series of goal-oriented, problem-solving activities aimed at the construction of a meaningful whole story. Our prior knowledge and experience of narratives, of genre conventions and of the social world create certain expectations and assumptions that we bring to interpreting a text. Much of the moment-by-moment processing involves us in making causal, temporal and spatial connections between events and interpreting stylistic elements for narrative meaning.

In analysing narration we can study how viewers put the story together by:

- formulating, testing and revising hypotheses on the basis of incoming information;
- making causal connections and inferences;
- reconstructing the temporal order and duration of events;
- filling in gaps in narrative time or causal logic;
- assessing the spatial frame of reference in which the story occurs;
- considering how space, décor, lighting, framing and other elements of style express human relationships.

Such problem-solving activities are more apparent when we watch crime, detective or mystery plots than when we watch melodramas (where enigmas are mainly based around the character's relationships and emotions). For example, Hitchcock's *Rear Window* (USA, dir. Hitchcock, 1954) is often used to study cinema spectatorship because we see events mainly from the vantage point of the chief protagonist, Jeff (see Figure 3.9), and we follow his attempt to reconstruct the murder story from his wheelchair. Like him, in voyeuristic fashion, we look out on to the apartment block opposite and try to piece together how the murder took place. The film is like a small-scale model of film spectatorship and it highlights viewers' activities with remarkable explicitness.

Figure 3.9 *A still from* Rear Window. *We see events from the point of view of the main character, Jeff, and we follow his inferences and predictions about who committed the murder and how*
Source: Ronald Grant Archive

The narration is mainly restricted to Jeff's point of view and this leads us to consider two of the most important aspects of narration: the range and the depth of information.

3.1 Range and depth of narrative information

This section shows how our interest in and responses to a film are manipulated by the flow of story information. The *range of knowledge* we receive may be more or less restricted. In *Rear Window* we only know what Jeff knows. *Restricted narration* is typical in detective films where the camera may even be tied to the detective all the way through the film (as in *The Big Sleep*). But narration is never entirely restricted. Unlike prose fiction, film seldom confines itself to what a single character knows, but distributes different kinds of knowledge between characters at different moments. This creates gaps in knowledge between characters on screen and between characters and spectator – and therefore suspense.

Melodramas tend to be very communicative about emotional states and use *unrestricted narration*. There are few major gaps in story information and little suspense as compared with detective films. Our curiosity is maintained by trying to predict how characters will react to events, and how relationships will develop. Melodramas (and often soap operas) employ forms of omniscient narration where the camera moves from one character to another, giving the spectator more knowledge than any one character. We see and know much more than the characters see or know. Suspense is created when we know something that a character does not know. When analysing a film's narration we ask: who knows what, how and when?

Narration is never completely unrestricted. There is always something that we do not know. Most films shift between restricted and unrestricted narration. In *Rear Window* we also see things from the point of view of other characters. We are given insights into what they see (point of view camera shot) or what they think (their subjective point of view may be communicated in dialogue). (This film is exceptional in the way it foregrounds the voyeuristic nature of film spectatorship.) A 'point of view' shot is one which is taken from approximately where the character's eyes would be and shows what the character sees. It is usually cut into a shot of what the character is looking at. For every scene and every shot we can ask: whose point of view is represented and how? The range of story information delivered by the plot creates a hierarchy of knowledge between viewers, characters and narrator (if there is one). We can ask, who knows more?

Study note *When you come to the Sequence Builder activity on the DVD-ROM, it will be important to think carefully about who knows what as this will have an impact on the way your narrative sequence works to create suspense or surprise.*

The narration also shifts in the *depth of knowledge* that it displays. Narrative depth refers to the degree of identification with characters that we are allowed and the depth of knowledge we are given about the thoughts and emotions of the characters. Narration may be plotted on a continuum of objectivity and subjectivity. We may only be privy to a character's outward, manifest behaviour or we may be allowed into a character's deepest emotional or mental states. Technical codes of camera positioning and the use of point of view shots play an important role in this respect.

Range and depth of knowledge are independent variables. For example, we may share an optical vantage point with a character, but we may not have access to her mental or emotional states or point of view. Hitchcock, for example, delights in giving us greater knowledge than the characters but, at times, restricts our vision to that of one character via point of view shots, creating huge suspense. The famous shower scene in his film *Psycho* (USA, dir. Hitchcock, 1960) combines rapid editing and restricted narration, rather than explicit violence, to create dramatic tension and suspense.

Manipulating depth of knowledge can have a variety of potent effects, increasing our identification with or distancing us from characters. At any moment in a film we can ask how deeply we are acquainted with the feelings, thoughts and plans of a character. While most conventional films use objective styles of narration (implying that there is no narrator), they nearly always include subjective point of view shots which give insight into the character's reactions. Some films use a narrator to present story information. A voice-over narration may be used or the narrator may appear in the film. The narrator may shift between a restricted and unrestricted range of knowledge, and greater or lesser degrees of subjectivity.

The extent to which a film exhibits recognition that it is addressing an audience is referred to as the 'degree of self-consciousness'. This might involve the cameo appearances of Hitchcock in his films or, in comic narratives, some direct verbal address to the audience. All film narration is self-conscious to some degree. Groucho Marx's comic asides to the audience are more so than most. Let us now see how range and depth of information can have tangible effects on viewers. How, in particular, does the flow of story information shape the pleasures and emotions that are triggered by melodramas?

3.2 Narration in melodrama

In this section we look at how melodramas such as *Imitation of Life* induce pathos and move (at least some of us) to tears? Why do we cry and why is crying pleasurable? One answer to this question is that melodramas place so many obstacles between the character's desire and its fulfilment that the anticipation of closure becomes an end in itself. But another line of reasoning suggests that the pleasures of melodrama derive from narrational strategies, particularly the unequal distribution of knowledge between characters, and between characters and viewers, rather than the desire for closure.

Steve Neale (1986) argues that melodramas are characterised by multiple misunderstandings and misidentifications (for example, in *Imitation of Life* Lora assumes Annie is Sarah Jane's nanny, Steve is assumed to be Lora's husband, but most importantly Lora simply does not 'know' her daughter's true feelings for Steve, nor does she 'know' Annie even after living with her for so long). There are also unexpected chance happenings (such as the encounter on the beach, which changes the lives of all involved), coincidences, missed meetings, startling revelations, failures to recognise something or someone, and last-minute rescues and reconciliations (for example, the pathos of the funeral scene). Events tend to lack strong causal connections as the forces of chance, fate and/or destiny exert their power over the protagonists. But omniscient narration means that we the spectators know more than any of the characters. The narration exploits the discrepancy in point of view between characters and spectators for emotional effect. We weep because we can see how they cannot prevent their own suffering – just as we cannot in our own lives. This knowledge can forge a powerful sense of identification with the characters.

Neale argues that two factors come into play at the point at which viewers tend to cry. Firstly, there is a coincidence of knowledge and point of view on the part of the spectator and a character. One of the most emotionally powerful scenes in *Imitation of Life* is the final meeting between Annie and Sarah Jane backstage at the nightclub. Annie asks if she can hold Sarah Jane in her arms once more and Sarah Jane relents. Annie tells her that she loves her and that nothing will ever change that. They embrace and their tears flow but the emotional climax is interrupted by the arrival of Sarah Jane's friend who takes Annie to be Sarah Jane's 'mammy' (maid). Sarah Jane acts as though her mother is her mammy and not her mother. Annie colludes with Sarah Jane's performance, pretending to be her mammy, and says a speedy farewell to Sarah Jane (calling her by her stage name Linda). In this goodbye shot only the viewer can see that Sarah Jane mouths 'Goodbye mama'. Not even her mother can see that she loves her and has finally acknowledged her. There is a coincidence of knowledge and point of view between Sarah Jane and the viewer, and this is the very moment when some viewers cry.

Secondly, important knowledge comes 'too late'. In the funeral scene, Sarah Jane's more public affirmation of her love for her mother comes 'too late' and this is a point at which some viewers cry. But why do some viewers find crying in the cinema so pleasurable? In order to explain this Steve Neal turns to psychoanalytical theories of narrative and film spectatorship. The narrative, he argues, sets up a fantasy structure based on an 'if only' scenario. If only Sarah Jane had recognised her self and her feelings earlier. The fantasy structure of many classic narrative films is motivated by the deep human desire for love (the main theme of the film) and this is powerfully symbolised by union with the mother. He goes on to argue that, as spectators, we take pleasure in acquiring power through our knowledge, but we are also powerless because we cannot intervene when fate strikes a blow – neither in the lives of the characters nor in our own lives. The unhappy ending is pleasurable, he argues, because it postpones the fulfilment of desire and because it suggests that 'tomorrow is another day'. Pleasure lies in the 'working through' of desire rather than in its fulfilment, and in the eternally deferred nature of wish fulfilment.

In this section we have seen how the unequal distribution and the range and depth of knowledge can have potent effects on viewers. In the next section we shall examine how what we see conveys important knowledge. In particular, we will explore how *mise-en-scène* in melodrama works to magnify the emotional universe and serves very important narrative functions. It is among the most significant techniques of storytelling in film and television.

3.3 *Mise-en-scène* in *Imitation of Life*

Mise-en-scène encompasses the use of lighting and colour, costumes, décor and props, performance and acting style, the spatial organisation of actors and objects and their relationship to one another. In analysing *mise-en-scène* it is difficult not to consider framing, camera movement and cinematographic decisions at the same time (Gibbs, 2002). Some refer to these as the mise-en-shot. The interaction of all of these elements make up the film's visual style. It encompasses what the viewer can see and the way in which we are encouraged to see it.

Mise-en-scène, like narration, gives but also withholds information about what has happened and what might happen. For the purposes of analysing *mise-en-scène* we can trace one element, lighting for example, and assess how it affects the narrative (or the politics of representation, see **Bennett, 2005**). We can examine patterns of colour, line and shape in the décor, and how its different elements attract our attention and shape our understanding of the story. If the iconic face or body of a star is a key ingredient of mise-en-scene, we can examine how the star's image (which is partly non-diegetic) reinforces narrative themes or affects the audience's expectations. For example, we could trace the whiteness and brightness of colour for Lora/Lana and Susie and compare the use of dark lugubrious colours to represent Annie and Sarah Jane. *Mise-en-scène* analysis is best done systematically to see how significant elements function both in their own right and in interaction with other elements to serve a narrative function.

Mise-en-scène analysis is crucial to understanding how information is conveyed in the process of watching a film. It establishes the relationship between seeing, telling and knowing. Through dialogue, characters tells us things, but facial expressions or a gesture, the use of colour, or décor, can show us things that contradict what we are told. *Mise-en-scène* can reveal important ideas or themes that might otherwise be difficult to convey, or express emotions that are so powerful that they cannot be contained within the film frame. *Imitation of Life* is remarkable for its rich visual style and for the way in which *mise-en-scène* is used for such purposes. In Reading 3.2 we concentrate on one particular sequence, although it exemplifies some of the stylistic strategies used across the film. The sequence takes place shortly after the last heart-breaking meeting between Annie and Sarah Jane, described above. Susie has stayed at home to look after Annie while Lora and Steve attend the screening of Lora's very successful Italian film. The sequence consists of five shots: an establishing shot, two close-ups of Annie and two close-ups of Susie.

Reading 3.2 Activity

Read the following extract from John Gibbs, *Mise-en-scène: Film Style and Interpretation* (Reading 3.2) and answer the following questions:

- How does *mise-en-scène* provide a silent commentary on the action?
- How do camera position and decor offer insights into relationships?
- How does *mise-en-scène* emphasise the narrative theme of 'performance' suggested by the title *Imitation of Life*?

Reading 3.2

John Gibbs, '*Mise-en-scène*: film style and interpretation'

Case study: *Imitation of Life*

The bedside sequence

When the scene commences, Susie is in full flow, relaying her version of events earlier in the evening to Annie. As the scene progresses Susie proceeds to unburden thoughts of her love for Steve, whilst Annie's responses delicately attempt to steer Susie toward the reality of her situation.

Susie: ... and I know mother didn't understand. Oh, it was *so* embarrassing. And poor Steve, I mean what could he do? She just swept over him like a tidal wave.

Annie: Now honey, it's only natural he'd like to go out with your mother, he always enjoyed her company. You remember that.

Susie: But it's different now. All summer long it's been Steve and me. (pause) Annie, you know don't you.

Annie: Know what?

Susie: That I'm in love with Steve. I've always been in love with Steve, and always will be.

Annie: Sure Susie, but like a little girl.

Susie: No, I don't think it even started like that. In a funny way I always knew. Every time I thought I liked a boy it was because he reminded me of Steve, and then I'd stop liking him because ... because he wasn't Steve.

The sequence begins with an establishing shot which is bisected vertically by a bedpost at the head of Annie's bed [see Figure 3.10]. To the left of this divide we can see Annie propped up by a pillow, her bed running toward the camera and the left hand side of the frame. To the right, in the foreground of the shot and facing the camera (although she turns around from time to time), sits Susie eating supper from a tray.

Figure 3.10 Imitation of Life: *the establishing shot*
Source: *Imitation of Life*

The right half of the image is colourful and cluttered. Susie is wearing a mauve jump-suit, a green lampshade extrudes from the upper right corner of the frame; in the distance is a bedside lamp. The table and tray are interposed between Susie and the camera, the chair at which she sits breaks up the space, the folds and pattern of the curtains form a backdrop. In contrast, the left half of the frame is bare and austere. The whites of the bed linen and the dark brown of the headboard, repeated in the wall and the shadow that falls across it above, are the predominant colours.

Annie, clearly unwell, lies very still, whereas Susie eats and chatters and gesticulates.

The comparative triviality of Susie's problems in relation to those suffered by Annie, apparent to the spectator from the narrative situation, is further evoked by the striking decisions of presentation. The fussiness of the right half of the frame contrasts with the bleakness of the left. The 'busy' decor associated with

Susie is evocative of her privileged adolescence as witnessed earlier in the film. Her appearance and her surroundings are entirely in keeping with her world of picnics, yellow sweaters, thoroughbreds, imagined kissing and boys. Annie, on the other hand, is mourning for her lost daughter and the stark setting suggests something of the magnitude of the emotion involved. Indeed, this is Annie's death bed and Annie is increasingly removed from material considerations. It is to Annie's immense credit that she has time for Susie.

The choices concerning décor and camera position make available to the audience an insight into the relationships between the characters in the house. The schism of the establishing shot conveys a tremendous sense of two adjacent but virtually incompatible worlds, two lives lived contiguous to one another, but in different milieux. The choice of a wide angle lens exaggerates the distance between the actors, and further enforces our sense of the boundary between the two. (At one moment Susie takes a glass of milk from Annie, which is rather startling, because the lens had suggested such a substantial space between them.)

The position of the characters in relation to each other and the camera is significant in another respect. Two shots where the audience can see both characters but one character has her or his back to the other are the stock-in-trade of melodrama, and the range of inflection that can be achieved through this simple arrangement is extremely variable. The most immediate consequence of such a framing is that the audience can read both characters' faces and so know more than either about how each is feeling. In this way the audience are privileged over the characters, and forms of dramatic irony can be rapidly established.

In this instance, the organisation of the visual field gives the spectator a more informed understanding of the scene than is available to Susie, both as a result of the blocking and the distinctions in décor. Not only can we see Annie and Susie all of the time, but also the division of the space which I have been describing can only be perceived by the audience. Indeed, viewed from another angle, the significance attributable to the decor would be lost (or changed).

The ideas introduced by the establishing shot are consolidated and developed in the images that follow. The other set-ups used in the early part of the scene – a close-up of Annie in bed along a similar axis, a slightly wider shot of Susie at ninety degrees – rigorously maintain the distinction in décor and colour present in the long-shot. Neither does the separation afforded by individual shots collapse our sense of the dislocation between the characters. Moreover, the close-ups of Annie enable us to perceive that which Susie does not notice [see Figure 3.11]. The first cut happens on the line 'Annie, you know don't you?', but we are offered a close-up of Annie that shows the degree of her suffering, rather than one of Susie, which would have served to make her declaration more emphatic.

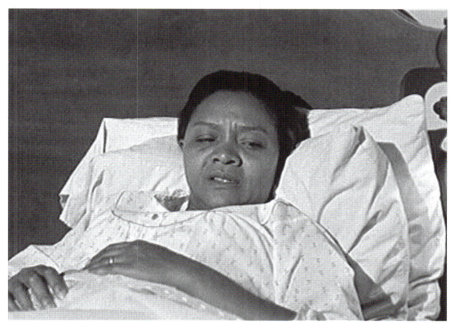

Figure 3.11 *Close-up of Annie (Juanita Moore)*
Source: *Imitation of Life*

Susie chatters on, paying little regard to Annie's remarks and, more importantly, oblivious to Annie's own situation. On the line, 'Sure Susie, but like a little girl', Annie turns away in obvious discomfort (there is an audible tightening of the breath) but Susie, looking away from Annie, fails to notice [see Figure 3.12]. Susie is so engrossed in her own conversation that she does not perceive that Annie has fallen asleep (or passed out?) for several moments. Returning from her reflection, Susie ascertains that Annie is asleep and turns out the light. She is about to leave the room when she hears the car pull up outside. She smiles indulgently as we watch her watching Lora and Steve through the window until, that is, she is dismayed to see them passionately embrace.

Figure 3.12 *Susie (Sandra Dee)*
Source: *Imitation of Life*

The pretensions of Susie's behaviour are clear to the audience: partly through our truer sense of the state of affairs between Lora, Steve and her; partly by the reversal of usual mother and daughter roles in this watching of the date returned home safely, and partly by the music which helps to cast the end of the scene in an ironic mode. The perception that Susie is *performing* the role of mother is one that is applicable to her behaviour throughout the sequence, however, and the way in which Sandra Dee performs Susie's romantic reflection and declamation enhances a suggestion of adolescent role play. She is trying out the role of the grown-up – and in doing so joins a whole cast of performers in the film.

Reading source

Gibbs, 2002, pp.84–8 ■■■

The split framing of the establishing shot and the decor set up a potent contrast between the bleakness surrounding Annie and the fussiness around Susie. It underscores the profound heartbreak that Annie is suffering compared with the more superficial trivialities of a teenage crush. Susie's emotional distance and her ignorance of Annie's problems are suggested by the wide-angle camera position and by the décor which emphasises the space between the characters. Décor is used throughout the film to convey a sense of the sharp boundaries between the domestic spaces in which Annie and Susie live. It is used to express the fundamentally exploitative, racialising, class relationship between 'master and slave' more vividly than can be done in words or in the seeming cosiness of the domestic set up.

The use of shots in which one character has their back to the other, leading to the failure of one to observe the important facial expressions, gestures and behaviour of the other, is common in this film and contributes to the omniscience of the narration typical of melodramas. The editing style also provides a silent commentary on the characters. Cutting to Annie, rather than focusing on Susie's face after her declaration of love for Steve, suggests to us the true depths of Annie's suffering.

Susie's acting style suggests that she is shallow and artificial, performing a social role; just like when, at a different moment in the film, Steve and Susie admonish Lora with the words 'Oh stop acting!' Susie is playing at being in love and being grown up. Lora is playing at being a loving mother. Sarah Jane is faking being white. The *mise-en-scène* lends powerful expression to the central theme of performance: of identities and feelings that are gendered, racialised and classed. Through the patterned use of mirrors the question of who we are and what we truly feel seems to turn back on us the viewers, creating an ironic distance between characters and viewers, mirror and screen. Douglas Sirk claimed that he would have made *Imitation of Life* for the title alone. It enabled him to explore both his vision of the relationship between art and reality and the difficulties of seeing life clearly, and the phrase from the Bible (1 Cor. 13: 12) that he liked to use to describe it – 'we see through a glass, darkly' (Sirk, quoted in Willemen, 1971).

The *mise-en-scène* vividly brings to life the thematic oppositions between the artifice and authenticity that were set up in the opening song:

What is life without the giving?

Without love, you're only living an imitation of life ...

A false creation, an imitation of life?

Annie, the love she gives, and her participation in the life of a local black community, are the repository of authenticity in the film. In contrast, Lora's performance in life and on stage is all artifice. It is also dependent on the back-stage role of Annie. Annie's kitchen space, compared with the palatial living room, the staircases and walkways, is a striking marker of their separate and bounded living spaces. These distinct spaces serve the function of balancing and connecting, in visual terms, the two stories. *Mise-en-scène* performs a kind of distancing effect – not from the character's emotions but in offering us a point of orientation from which to see and evaluate action – inaccessible to the characters themselves (Gibbs, 2002, p.95). *Mise-en-scène* expresses not only what the characters cannot say but also the film's complex structure. We could say that much of this story lies in the showing not the telling.

In this final section we have explored how narration involves controlling the flow of story information and how the range and depth of knowledge to which we are given access has very important consequences for how we, as viewers, engage in the process of story construction. This is a highly active process that engages our minds as well as our emotions. It does so through the way in which the plot presents and distributes information, often unequally, between characters on screen and between characters and us as viewers. Film and television narratives oscillate between telling us and showing us things and that is why we have explored in some detail *mise-en-scène* and *mise-en-shot*. Melodramas usually make exceptionally good use of *mise-en-scène* and carry the emotional excess that spills out from the characters and narrative. While it is useful to examine particular elements of *mise-en-scène*, it is the interaction of all the features of narration that make films such a vivid and captivating experience.

4   Conclusion

This chapter has woven a narrative of it own. We started out with a comic narrative (a joke) and ended up with a melodramatic one. Both narratives depict relations of power based on 'race', ethnicity, class and gender. They refer particularly to the kind of master/slave relations that characterised colonial (English–Irish) and slave (US white–black) relations in the past, and which continue to leave their traces today. They are both tightly structured narratives that dramatise these conflicts and go some way to challenging stereotypical ways of thinking. Both joke and melodrama valorise Irish and black cultures in contrast to the official English or WASP (white anglo-saxon Protestant) culture. But neither narrative enacts a transformation in fundamental power relations in their narrative resolution and closure. In other words, nothing much has changed except that some of us may have laughed and some cried (that is if you have managed to see the film). Both narratives are constructed in ways that try to create such an impact.

As societies change so do narratives. The joke and melodrama make sense at the moment of telling. *Imitation of Life* was designed to make sense to US audiences in 1959 and clearly it did. It attracted large black film audiences (Willemen, 1971). The Irish joke is meaningful among second and third generation Irish people today in a climate where the positive assertion of ethnic identity and political correctness is valued. Narratives circulate as long as they are meaningful to their receivers and then they either change to correspond to existing values (as the tale of Cinderella did, see Section 1) or disappear. The tales of suffering and of celebrity women: Lora/Lana Turner and Marilyn Monroe, Cinderella and Annie, have featured in several narratives considered in this chapter. You may now be able to trace structural similarities between them but we can also see how, through their varied re-tellings, they assume different meanings and are likely to have different impacts at different moments.

Media stories operate according to a commercial aesthetic – one that tells stories in order to entertain to make profits. But should the pleasures we derive from cinema mean that film stories cannot be considered as works of art to be analysed with the same scrutiny and rigour as the narratives of great novelists? The forms of narrative analysis encountered in this chapter have taken us a long way towards replying in the affirmative.

This chapter has offered you a set of tools for narrative analysis that you can apply to a wide range of media texts. They are not intended to be prescriptive but can be used in a flexible manner to analyse how narrative texts work. The distinction between story and plot has helped us see how narrative texts need to be analysed from the vantage point of both the storyteller and the story-receiver. We have seen how the different elements that form a narrative – causality, time and space – operate together to create meaning, and how they relate to story and plot. We have also seen how mapping narrative structures can be a rewarding exercise. It reveals how narratives that appear to be very different in fact share certain basic features. It can show us how our engagement with narrative is conventional and patterned, so we need to watch out for how stories can impose as well as create certain meanings – including meanings that serve the interests of power. We have examined narration as a dynamic process that hooks us into its forward-thrusting movement and cues us to perform a series of purposeful and compelling story construction activities.

Analysing narrative structure and narrational processes are complementary activities, not mutually exclusive approaches. Analysing narrative structures requires an essentially static lens, while studying processes of narration captures the moment-by-moment activities in which viewers engage. In analysing film texts we also need to consider the use of specific film techniques. *Mise-en-scène* analysis is fruitful and fun. It gets to grips with the important details of how information is conveyed, what we see and how we are encouraged to see it. It is hoped that in using these tools your understanding of the narratives of the world, as well as the abundant pleasures that they bring and in which we all share, will be enriched.

DVD-ROM

Now that you have finished reading Chapter 3, work through the Narrative activities in the Chapter Activities area of the *Analysing Media Texts* DVD-ROM. ▪▪▪

Further reading

Bordwell, D. and Thompson, K. (2000) *Film Art: An Introduction*, New York, McGraw-Hill. A very detailed introduction to analysing film narratives – includes essay examples.

Chatman, S. (1978) *Story and Discourse*, Ithaca, NY, Cornell University. A different kind of approach to that proposed by David Bordwell.

Ellis, J. (1992) *Visible Fictions* (revised edition), London, Routledge. This book has very useful chapters on narration in film and television.

Lacey, N. (2000) *Narrative and Genre: Key Concepts in Media Studies*, Basingstoke and New York, Palgrave. An accessible introduction to the analysis of media narratives with lots of worked examples.

References

Aristotle (1920) *On the Art of Poetry.* (trans. I. Bywater), Oxford, Clarendon Press.

Aristotle (1996) *Poetics* (trans. M. Heath), London, Penguin.

Barthes, R. (1997/1966) 'Introduction to the structural analysis of narratives' (trans. S. Heath) in *Images, Music, Text*, London, Fontana.

Bennett, T. (2005) 'The media sensorium: cultural technologies, the senses and society' in Gillespie, M. (ed.) *Media Audiences*, Maidenhead, Open University Press/The Open University (Book 2 in this series).

Bordwell, D. (1985) *Narration in the Fiction Film*, Madison, WI, The University of Wisconsin Press.

Bordwell, D. and Thompson, K. (1990) *Film Art: An Introduction*, New York, McGraw-Hill.

Chatman, S. (1978) *Story and Discourse*, Ithaca, NY, Cornell University.

Gibbs, J. (2002) *Mise-en-scène: Film Style and Interpretation*, London and New York, Wallflower.

Gillespie, M. (2005) 'Television drama and audience ethnography' in Gillespie, M. (ed.) *Media Audiences*, Maidenhead, Open University Press/The Open University (Book 2 in this series).

Hesmondhalgh, D. (ed.) (2005) *Media Production*, Maidenhead, Open University Press/The Open University (Book 3 in this series).

Neale, S. (1986) 'Melodrama and Tears', *Screen*, vol.27, no.6, pp.6–23.

Propp, V. (1968/1928) *Morphology of the Folktale* (2nd edn) (trans. L. Scott), Austin, TX, University of Texas Press.

Todorov, T. (1977/1971) *The Poetics of Prose* (trans. R. Howard), Ithaca, NY, Cornell University Press.

Warner, M. (1995) *From the Beast to the Blonde: On Fairy Tales and Their Tellers*, London, Chatto and Windus.

Willemen, P. (1971) 'Distanciation and Douglas Sirk', *Screen*, vol.12, no.2, pp.63–7.

Discourse analysis and content analysis

Chapter 4

David Hesmondhalgh

Contents

1   Introduction

This chapter explores two contrasting methods of textual analysis. Both of them build on the methods and concepts addressed in the previous chapters. The first method, discourse analysis, does so by paying special attention to media *language*. Semiotics, explored in Chapter 1, is an approach that initially grew out of linguistics (the study of language) but, paradoxically, it has been used primarily to help us to think more carefully about visual images and how they convey meaning. Strangely, this has resulted in a situation in which media language has, as it were, been left out of the picture. Similarly, genre and narrative, explored in Chapters 2 and 3, are both concepts that can be applied fruitfully to those media based primarily around the spoken and written word, as well as to audio-visual media such as film and television. Yet studies that focus on genre and narrative have paid relatively little attention to language-based media, such as radio and newspapers, and have tended to neglect the specifically linguistic ways in which such media as film and television convey meaning, alongside their use of images. Discourse analysis is an important means of filling this language gap in analysing media texts.

The second method, content analysis, builds in a somewhat different way upon the other concepts and methods examined in this book. Whereas some forms of textual analysis dig deep into the meanings of a particular text or of a small number of texts, content analysis allows us to look across large numbers of texts. It is a *quantitative* method: that is, it involves counting and measuring quantities of items such as words, phrases or images. *Qualitative* methods, such as discourse, genre and narrative analysis, by contrast tend to be based on interpretation, rather than on such measurement. (The quantitative/qualitative distinction is a simple but fundamental one in the social sciences and the humanities.)

The most immediate benefit of quantitative methods such as content analysis is that they offer greater potential to *generalise* than do qualitative ones. For example, if I wanted to make an argument about the way in which UK television news represents famine in Africa, then I could analyse a single news report, and show how it uses genre conventions and narratives; and I could use concepts from semiotics to unpack the often latent and/or unintended meanings of the report. As we shall see shortly, we could use discourse analysis to think about the use of language in the news report. But it would be very difficult to draw any firm conclusions about how famine is represented in television news *in general* using these qualitative methods. I would need to analyse sufficient examples of UK television news reports to make it possible to say, with some degree of validity, that UK television news reports about famine during a particular period had certain features rather than others. If successful, though, this would be important and might convince more people of the benefits or problems of famine reporting than would merely focusing on one report, or on a small number of reports, in depth.

Quantitative studies can reveal *recurring* processes of representation that affect our values and beliefs across a large number of cases. This means that they can sometimes have a powerful effect on opinion and policy. Quantitative methods such as content analysis (content analysis is by far the most significant quantitative method of textual analysis of media) can therefore be very useful and important in media studies. However, like all methods of research, quantitative methods have their limitations, and we shall explore these limitations in this chapter as well.

But why examine these two distinct approaches – discourse and content analysis – in the same chapter? The answer is that looking at discourse and content analysis together provides the opportunity to think about the differences between quantitative and qualitative methods in some depth, and to consider how different methods and techniques can focus on different kinds of meaning. As we shall see, discourse analysis tends to be better at revealing *latent* or hidden meanings, while content analysis is better suited to examining *manifest* or more readily apparent meanings. This is an important distinction to bear in mind while thinking about media texts.

The structure of the chapter is as follows. Section 2 will introduce discourse analysis and some of the basic qualitative tools it uses by drawing on two studies: one from broadcasting, one from newspapers. Section 3 will introduce content analysis by examining a study of representations of 'race' and poverty in US news magazines. Section 4 will address how we might evaluate accounts of the media, especially (given the present context), accounts based on textual analysis. One of the criteria we might use for evaluating these accounts is empirical adequacy: that is, whether theory and evidence are used adequately to support conclusions. To investigate what might constitute adequate evidence in content analysis, we will examine the study of news magazines. This also allows us to look at the question of how to do content analysis and how to carry it out effectively. However, we shall also see in this section that different research traditions understand empirical adequacy in different ways, and this takes us back to the split between quantitative and qualitative methods. This split is a key issue in this chapter as there has tended to be a division of labour between those carrying out quantitative and qualitative media research. Section 5 will demonstrate that discourse analysis and content analysis (qualitative and quantitative methods respectively) can, in principle, be combined and illustrates this via a discussion of the genre of daytime talk shows, and the programme *Trisha Goddard* in particular.

2 Discourse analysis

'Discourse' is a term that is used in a variety of ways in linguistics and other social sciences. We can distinguish between two main uses of the term. One, predominant in language studies, sees discourse as 'social action and interaction, people interacting together in real social situations' (Fairclough, 1995, p.18). That is, the focus is on language as it is used. The second use of the term is very much associated with the work of the French cultural historian and social theorist Michel Foucault (1926–1984, see Foucault, 1977), and has very little to do with linguistics. This second use understands 'a discourse as a social construction of reality, a form of knowledge' (Fairclough, 1995, p.18) which determines what is knowable, sayable and doable in a particular historical context. Fairclough's approach to discourse subsumes both these uses and is intended to bring them together by analysing language use in some detail (in conformity with the first use of the term), but always in relation to social and cultural processes (the emphasis in the second use).

Discourse analysis is only one of a number of approaches which offer the means to analyse language in social use. Not only is discourse analysis just one means of analysing media language, there are different kinds of discourse analysis too. There is no space here to deal with anything approaching the full range of approaches to discourse (Titscher et al., 2000, provide a wide-ranging survey). We concentrate here on approaches to media discourse developed by the UK linguist Norman Fairclough and the Dutch linguist Teun van Dijk. They are important in the present context because they attempt to draw connections between the use of language and the exercise of social power. For this reason, their work is often labelled 'critical discourse analysis' – because it claims to be more critical of language as it is used socially than are some other types of discourse and linguistic analysis. (There are some differences between the approaches of Fairclough and van Dijk to critical discourse analysis, but in the present context these can be seen as relatively minor. Both writers have also written widely about non-media examples of language use.)

2.1 Fairclough: representations, identities and relations

Let us now look at some critical discourse analysis in action. In his book *Media Discourse* (1995), Norman Fairclough explains the usefulness of analysing the language of media texts. He argues that such analysis can illuminate three sets of questions about media output:

1   How is the world (events, relationships, etc.) *represented*?

2   What *identities* are set up for those involved in the programme or story (reporters, audiences, 'third parties' referred to or interviewed)?

3   What *relationships* are set up between those involved (for example, reporter–audience, expert–audience or politician–audience relationships)?

Fairclough goes on to say that a 'useful working assumption is that any part of any text ... will be simultaneously representing [the world], setting up identities, and setting up relations' (1995, p.5). In Reading 4.1, Fairclough analyses two examples of media language using these categories of representation, identities and relations.

Reading 4.1 Activity

Read the following two extracts from Fairclough's book *Media Discourse*. The two examples that Fairclough analyses are:

1   An edition of an ITV current affairs programme called *This Week*. This edition was entitled 'Vigilante!' and was broadcast in the UK in 1992.

2   An extract from the BBC Radio 4 news programme *Today*, also broadcast in the UK in 1992. (*Today* is broadcast every morning from Monday to Saturday, and is the BBC's 'flagship' radio news programme.)

As you read the two extracts, make brief notes about what Fairclough's argument is concerning the most striking characteristic of each extract.

Reading 4.1

Norman Fairclough, 'Media and language: setting an agenda'

This Week

The programme opens with a 'trailer' which gives brief versions of the vigilante stories to be covered, followed by the usual *This Week* opening visual sequence and signature tune, then the programme title 'Vigilante!' imposed on a still picture of a silhouetted man carrying what appears to be an axe handle. My extract comes after this. On the left I have given a rough representation of visual images in the extract, and on the right the language (reporter voice-over).

IMAGES	LANGUAGE
Pictures of hills and valleys, sound of choir.	As the coalmines of South Wales fall silent, the blackened hills and valleys grow green again. It's a picture of peace.
Groups of people converge on a house, shouting.	But in the village of Penwyn, in July, an ugly scene was played out following the violent death of an elderly spinster.
Crowd in front of houses, gestures and shouts.	When two teenage girls from the neighbourhood were charged with murder, a mob of several hundred local people converged on the houses where the parents of the accused lived.
Missiles picked up and thrown at windows, sounds of breaking glass, crowd shouting and cheering.	(*Long pause filled with shouting.*) The dead woman's complaints of harassment had apparently gone unheeded. The crowd were enraged by reports she'd been so brutally killed that she could only be identified by her fingerprints. (*Long pause filled with shouting.*) A shower of missiles drove the families from their homes. The police could do nothing but help them to safety.

This extract takes one step further the tendency in [an earlier example taken from a current affairs programme about nuclear fuel] for reporter and audience identities and relations to be on the entertainer–consumer model. The genre is past-event narrative, and the story is told through a combination of words and what the programme identifies as a filmed reconstruction of the incident. The extract, and indeed the programme as a whole, is on the borderline between information and entertainment, and between fact and fiction. The visual narrative of the film, in which the crowd is played by actors, is dramatic fiction.

The images have primacy over the words in the sense that the events related happen first visually (e.g. we see a missile thrown before we hear *a shower of missiles*). (See Barthes, 1977, and van Leeuwen, 1991, on variable relationships between words and images.) The linguistic account provides an interpretation of the images, identifying the people in the crowd, the house and its inhabitants, but also shifting between narrating events and providing setting and background for them, often in the same sentence. An important part of this is providing explanations of the crowd's behaviour.

There are also apparent inconsistencies between words and images. The images show, first, groups of angry-looking people walking purposefully along shouting, then a crowd of angry people shouting and gesticulating in front of the lighted window of a house, then some of them hurling missiles at the window, and glass breaking. Responsibility for the violence is clear and unmitigated in the film. In the linguistic account, responsibility is less clearly attributed, and is mitigated. There are just three clauses (simple sentences) which recount the incident itself. What is interesting is both the way these are formulated, and the way they are positioned in the account. The first (*an ugly scene was played out*) is vague about who did what to whom, the third (*a shower of missiles drove the families from their homes*) transforms the action of throwing missiles into an entity, a shower of missiles, and does not indicate who actually did it. Only in the second (*a mob of several hundred local people converged on the houses*) is the crowd represented as actually taking action, and then it is 'converging on' (which implies a *controlled* action that does not entirely square with the behaviour of a 'mob') rather than 'attacking' the house.

What I'm suggesting is that the linguistic account is rather restrained in blaming the crowd. True, it is referred to damningly as 'a mob', but two sentences later it is referred to more neutrally as 'the crowd'. What is significant about the positioning of these event clauses is that they are separated by background explanatory clauses. This both slows down the story and reduces the impact of violence; it also mitigates the actions of the crowd by framing them with a great deal of interpretative, explanatory material. There is, in short, ambivalence in the representation here which accords, I think, with an ambivalence in the programme as a whole: it does not wish to defend unlawful violence, but it represents the vigilantes as normally decent people frustrated by the ineffectiveness of the law. The notion of 'good television' perhaps favours the image of frightening violence in the film, which is unambivalent, but which can be partly 'balanced' by mitigating language. Once again, there is a tension between information and entertainment.

[...]

Today

My final example is taken from the *Today* programme which is broadcast every weekday morning on BBC Radio 4. The particular programme I am using was broadcast during the 1992 general election campaign (8 April 1992). The presenter, Brian Redhead (BR), is asking representatives of each of the three main political parties (Conservative, Labour, Liberal Democrat) why an imaginary 'floating voter' should support them.

BR   now our floating voter turns to you Brian Gould [*sic*] and he says look (BG: yeah) I don't really fancy another Conservative government I think we've had enough of that but I can't really bring myself to vote for you because you've been out of office for so long you haven't got the experience if you get in the City might say do this lot know enough to run the country I'm nervous that a vote for you would mean a vote for some kind of flight from the pound.

(answer from Brian Gould, question from BR to Des Wilson, and answer from Des Wilson omitted)

BR   Des Wilson thank you now. imagine this floating voter actually is a mate of all three of you. knows you personally. and has sat up he's a different bloke altogether this one's been here through the whole election he's listened to every blooming broadcast (one of panel: lucky chap) he's fed up to the back teeth (one of panel: haven't we all). and he rings you up and says the same question to each of you and I just want a quick answer from each if you would. he says. hey Chris. e:m. your campaign has been dreadful. I mean you've just underestimated the intelligence of the electorate and particularly of me. what would you why did you get it wrong

Conversationalization is much more marked in this case. The presenter is constructed as an ordinary bloke talking to ordinary people, sharing with them a common 'lifeworld' (Habermas 1984), a commonsense world of ordinary experience. One conversational feature is the direct representation of the talk of others, including an attempt to imitate the voice of the (real or imaginary) original. Indeed, this whole item is built around the presenter's simulation of the voice of the floating voter. Conversationalization is also realized in a variety of linguistic features. Most obvious are items of colloquial vocabulary (*fancy, mate, bloke, blooming*) and the colloquial idiom *fed up to the back teeth*. Notice also that *altogether* is used in a distinctively conversational way, in close association with *different,* placed after a noun, meaning 'completely'. The extract includes the colloquial use of the demonstrative pronoun *this* to refer to someone previously mentioned (e.g. *imagine this floating voter actually is a mate of all three of you*). There is also a feature of conversational narrative in the use of narrative present tense (e.g. from earlier in this interview, *he comes back to you Chris Patten and he says*).

References

Barthes, R. (1977) *Image, Music, Text* (trans. S. Health), London, Fontana.

Habermas, J. (1984) *Theory of Communicative Action, Vol.1*
(trans. T. McCarthy), London, Heinemann.

Van Leeuwen, T. (1991) 'Conjunctive structure in documentary film and television', *Continuum*, vol.5, no.1, pp.76–114.

Reading source

Fairclough, 1995, pp.5–10 ▪ ▪ ▪

In Fairclough's analysis of *This Week*, his main argument is that there is a tension between information and entertainment evident in the programme, and that this is apparent not only in the use of dramatic re-enactment, but in the language of the extract, which is ambivalent about the use of violence by the crowd of 'vigilantes'. Note that Fairclough makes his argument here by analysing the words used over the images in very close detail. In particular, he analyses the report's vagueness about who did what, by scrutinising not only the words used, but the sequence in which they are used and their relationship to other forms of words that were not chosen.

One example is 'an ugly scene was played out'. Fairclough observes the way in which the form of words used here avoids making clear who is doing what. We might recall here Fairclough's earlier point about how uses of media language always suggest a set of *identities* and *relations*. The identity constructed for the 'vigilantes' is, in Fairclough's words, 'normally decent people frustrated by the ineffectiveness of the law'. Furthermore, Fairclough is suggesting that, by not condemning the actions of the 'vigilantes' and by providing so much explanatory material about their actions, the programme is allowing the audience to indulge in the spectacle of (re-enacted) violence as a kind of entertainment. This reveals his view of one important set of relations in the piece: the relationship between the programme and its audience is one in which members of the audience are addressed as consumers, to be entertained, perhaps more than as citizens who need to be informed about such important matters of crime, the causes of crime, and the forms that punishment should take.

In his analysis of the *Today* programme, Fairclough argues that the exchanges demonstrate 'conversationalization' – the use of ordinary conversation in areas of social life in which it was not previously apparent. There is more emphasis on vocabulary than in the analysis of the other extract: Fairclough points to particular words such as 'fancy', 'mate' and 'blooming'. But he is again concerned with syntax (the structure of language), such as 'different bloke altogether' and also with tense, such as the use in English of the present tense to tell a story about the past: 'he rings you up and he says' etc., a use that Fairclough interprets, surely correctly, as conversational rather than formal.

Study note *For an example of a news report that demonstrates 'conversationalization', see the news bulletin in the Viewing Room area of the DVD-ROM,* Analysing Media Texts.

We have seen, then, that the analysis of media language in critical discourse analysis involves paying very close attention to specific examples of language use. However, it is important to realise that the point of such close analysis is not only to reveal the specifically linguistic properties of media texts. It is also to work from this to the sociocultural implications of the media. In this particular case, Fairclough does so by recapping two tensions affecting contemporary media language: between information and entertainment, but also between private and public. This last tension is apparent, says Fairclough, in the way in which a private conversational idiom is brought into public forums such as political news broadcasts.

He then proceeds to relate these tensions to two key tendencies in news and current affairs media. The first, building on his analysis of the *Today* programme, is that such media are becoming more *conversationalised*. The second, signalled in his analysis of *This Week*, is that such media are moving increasingly in the direction of entertainment – to become *marketised*. By 'marketised', Fairclough means the tendency for media to operate more and more on a market basis: that is, on the basis of producing media products for exchange, with profit making a primary motive. He then makes a further move, which is to relate these tendencies to the broader question of power: 'the question of how the mass media affect and are affected by power relations within the social system, including relations of class, gender, and ethnicity, and relations between particular groups like politicians or scientists and the mass of the population' (Fairclough, 1995, p.12). For Fairclough, the increasing construction of audiences as consumers to be entertained undermines the idea of the media audience as a public, as a collectivity of individuals who can affect the social and political realm, and so attention and energy are diverted away from social and political issues. This, in Fairclough's view, helps protect existing relations of power from serious challenge.

However, Fairclough is more ambivalent about the relationship between conversationalisation and issues of power. He asks: '[D]o conversationalized discourse practices manifest a real shift in power relations in favour of ordinary people, or are they to be seen as merely a strategy on the part of those with power to more effectively recruit people as audiences and manipulate them socially and politically?'

(Fairclough, 1995, p.13.) Taking the example in which presenter Bryan Redhead adopts the voice of a floating voter, who in turn adopts the perspective of 'the City' (by which he means the international financial institutions that operate in the part of London known as 'the City', equivalent to 'Wall Street' in the USA), Fairclough suggests that in some cases conversationalisation can help to 'naturalise' ways of thinking that favour the interests of the powerful. But Fairclough also points to ways in which conversationalisation can serve to democratise certain forms of expert knowledge, for example those surrounding technology or medicine; and to how, in politics, the widespread adoption of conversational idiom by powerful actors such as politicians can have unexpected consequences. As Fairclough puts it, if those who are relatively powerful 'claim to be ordinary, they may find themselves evaluated as ordinary people and found wanting, and unable to resort to traditional resources of political mystique and charisma to protect themselves' (Fairclough, 1995, p.14; see also **Evans, 2005**, on related issues concerning politics and celebrity).

It is worth noting the way in which Fairclough proceeds in his analysis. He begins from a small piece of ordinary language use, but then makes connections between these individual, 'micro' (small-scale) uses of language, and much broader 'macro' questions concerning the arrangements of authority and power in society. He does this in two ways. Firstly, he uses a series of 'meso' (middle) level issues – his three key concepts of representation, identities and relations, which he says can be applied to all language use. Secondly, he uses more specific middle-level concepts such as, in the cases analysed above, marketisation and conversationalisation. Not all linguistic analysis attempts to make these connections between micro and macro issues. In fact a great deal of linguistic analysis confines itself to studies that throw light on the internal structure of a particular language, rather than on the connections between language, power and society. So Fairclough and other advocates of critical discourse analysis are perhaps the most useful language analysts to draw upon when we are trying to consider the constantly changing role of the media in societies characterised by stark inequalities of power between different social groups. This usefulness, along with more strategies for analysis, can be demonstrated using another case study.

2.2 Van Dijk: 'us' and 'them' in the press

In Reading 4.2, Teun van Dijk analyses a report from the UK newspaper *The Sun* from 1989. Although this is an old newspaper report, it deals with an issue that is topical in the twenty-first century – immigration – and does so in a way that is still prevalent in newspapers today. Van Dijk examines the piece from *The Sun* (see Figure 4.1) in the context of 'the new racism'. A number of commentators have argued since the 1980s that traditional forms of racism, based on explicit beliefs in white superiority, have been giving way to new forms of racism, which are more subtle than traditional forms, and which in many cases (though by no means all) rely on discourse rather than on violence and segregation: 'they are expressed, enacted and confirmed by text and talk, such as everyday conversations, board meetings, job interviews, policies, laws, parliamentary debates ... movies, TV programmes and news reports in the press, among hundreds of other genres' (van Dijk, 2000, p.34). This makes it all the more important, then, to analyse such discourse in detail, including media discourse (the movies, television programmes and news reports that van Dijk mentions), in order to unpick its significance for ethnic inequality in society.

Two points should be made as a prelude to this reading. Firstly, the terms 'black', 'white' and 'race' are extremely problematic. Many would see such terms as themselves the product of very dubious ways of lumping together different ethnic groups and characteristics. You should assume that these terms have invisible quotation marks around them in what follows. Like van Dijk, I am using the terms because they are widely used in society as a whole, not because I think they are fruitful, fair or accurate ways of talking about ethnic difference. Secondly, while 'non-white' individuals and groups are undoubtedly capable of racist sentiment towards white people, in nearly all cases they have much less power to act upon those sentiments in a systematic way than do whites. One example of this is the media themselves. British daily newspapers are owned and staffed almost entirely by white people, but concern themselves a great deal with the representation of various non-white groups. This is why the discussion of racism in van Dijk's work and in this chapter concentrates on white racism.

Reading 4.2 Activity

Now read the following extract from Teun A. van Dijk's work, 'New(s) racism: a discourse analytical approach'. As you go through the passage, make a brief note of the main 'tools' van Djik uses to analyse media language (van Dijk indicates these by using bold italics). Using a dictionary where appropriate, try to note down what these terms mean.

Reading 4.2

Teun A. van Dijk, 'New(s) racism: a discourse analytical approach'

The news report we analyse is taken from the British tabloid the *Sun* of 2 February 1989. It is presented as a 'News Special', which suggests not only that it is 'news' but also that the *Sun* probably has done some 'investigative reporting' of its own. It is signed by John Kay and Alison Bowyer. The article deals with 'illegal immigration' and police raids of various establishments where 'illegal immigrants' were arrested. Given the *Sun's* circulation, millions of British readers may have seen this article.

The article takes up nearly a whole page, with three pictures of 'raided' restaurants on the left, with a band on the picture saying 'RAIDED'. In the middle of the article there is a figure with statistics of 'illegal immigration' headlined 'HOW THE ILLEGALS TOTAL HAS SHOT UP'.

Over the full width of the page there is a huge banner headline saying: **BRITAIN INVADED BY AN ARMY OF ILLEGALS**

Let us begin our analysis, quite appropriately, with this not exactly unobtrusive headline. Theoretically, headlines express the major topic of an article. In this case, the topic is 'illegal immigration' more generally, and not (as in most news items) a specific event. This is also the reason why this is a 'News Special', and not a normal news report. News specials may deal with an issue, and in that respect are more like background articles.

In our analysis, we shall print theoretical terms in bold italic, so as to highlight what kind of analytical concept is being used in the description. Implications and interpretations are printed in italic, and relate to the structures of news on ethnic affairs dealt with above. Instead of dealing with each phenomenon separately, we study them in an integrated way for various fragments, since they often are closely related. Words used in the article quoted in our running text are signalled by quotation marks.

The most obvious property of this headline is its ***rhetoric***, as is common in tabloid headlines, namely, the ***hyperbolic*** use of ***metaphors***. Thus, entering Britain is conceptualized as an 'invasion', which is a common negative metaphor to represent immigration, and the immigrants are described with a metaphor of the same military ***register***, namely, as an army. Obviously, such metaphors are hardly innocent, and the use of military metaphors implies that immigrants are both *violent* and a *threat*. We have seen that violence and threat [are] among the main properties of the meaning of news discourse on immigrants. However, the violence and threat [are] not merely those of some individuals coming in, but [are] suggested to be *massive* and *organized*, as in the case for an army. Moreover, invasion does not merely imply a violent act, but also a massive threat, namely a massive threat from abroad. The target of this threat is Britain, which is ***topicalized*** in the headline (it occurs in first position of the headline and the article), so that it is highlighted as the victim of the foreign army. On the other hand the ***passive sentence*** construction emphasizes the 'news' by putting the 'invasion by the army of illegals' as the *comment* of the sentence. Note, finally, that only one dimension of the immigrants is selected in naming them, namely, that they are 'illegal'. This *lexicalization* is adopted also in the mainstream press in most European countries and North America to describe undocumented immigrants. Beside the massive violence of their entry, immigrants are thus also *associated* with breaking the law, and hence implicitly with *crime*.

It needs no further comment that at various levels of the structure of this headline, immigrants are being described very negatively according to the third main topic of ethnic issues, namely 'They are a Threat to Us'. But even the notion of Threat is not strong enough, and here further emphasized by stereotypical hyperbolic metaphors used to describe an Outside Threat.

Let us now consider some other fragments of this 'News Special'. The lead, printed over three columns, reads as follows:

1   BRITAIN is being swamped by a tide of illegal immigrants so desperate for a job that they will work for a pittance in our restaurants, cafes and nightclubs.

As usual, leads express the macrostructure of the text, and thus further specify the main topic expressed in the headline. Whereas the headline further abstracts from 'illegals' working in restaurants and other establishments, and describes Britain in general, here further information about the more specific location or targets of the 'foreign army' is given. However, also in this lead sentence, Britain is *topicalized* as the point of focus, the target of the army, and thus not syntactically marked by the passive sentence, but also further graphically emphasized by the use of *capital letters*.

Then the other standard *metaphor* is being used to negatively describe the arrival of foreigners, namely, that of threatening water, namely, by 'swamped' and 'tide'. The 'swamp' metaphor is well known in Britain, because it was used by Margaret Thatcher in 1979 when she said she understood ordinary British people being 'rather swamped' by people with an alien culture. Again, the actors are being described as being 'illegal', a form of *rhetorical repetition* that further emphasizes that the immigrants break the law and are hence criminals.

There follows an apparent local rupture in the dominant negative meanings in the characterization of the immigrants when they are being described as 'desperate'. Such a description usually implies empathy, and such *empathy* is inconsistent with a description of immigrants in the threatening terms of an 'army' or a 'tide'. However, the rest of the sentence shows that this description is not necessarily one of empathy, but rather explains why the immigrant workers are prepared to work for a 'pittance'. This implies that they are also an *economic threat* to the country, because they thus easily are able to compete against 'legal' workers. This implied meaning is consistent with the current prejudice about foreigners that 'they take away our jobs'.

Finally, notice the first explicit use of an ***ingroup designator***, the ***possessive pronoun*** 'our', thus establishing a clear contrast between Us and Them. That such a use is emphasizing ingroup–outgroup polarization is also obvious from the fact that the rest of the article also speaks about restaurants owned by foreigners or immigrants. That is, the restaurants or other establishments are not literally 'ours' but 'belong to Britain' in a broader, nationalist sense.

> 2　(a) Immigration officers are being overwhelmed with work. (b) Last year 2,191 'illegals' were nabbed and sent back home. (c) But there are tens of thousands more, slaving behind bars, cleaning hotel rooms and working in kitchens. (d) And when officers swoop on an establishment, they often find huge numbers of unlawful workers being employed.

In this first sentence after the lead, other participants are being introduced in the report, namely 'immigration officers', again topicalized in a passive sentence, and again, as in the headline and the lead as victims, but this time of being 'overwhelmed by work'. This verb is a more subdued, but still quite strong, concept of the series established by 'invaded' and 'swamped', and ***implies*** *powerlessness* against the force, or in this case, the sheer size of the number of 'illegals'.

The relevance of this implication becomes obvious in the next sentence, which argumentatively provides the statistical 'facts' that prove the amount of work. The same is true for the included figure that literally illustrates the rising number by a steeply climbing line, and the caption how the 'illegals total has shot up', a metaphor that also is borrowed from the domain of violence (as is 'army' and 'invaded'). Rhetorically, this well-known ***number game*** of much immigration reporting in the media, does not imply that these numbers are both necessarily incorrect. Rather they signal subjectivity and hence credibility, whereas the numbers themselves imply the size of the threat. And if a modest number like '2,191' should prove to be a weak case for the use of 'invaded' and 'army' and 'swamp', the reporters speak of 'tens of thousands', thus fully engaging in the speculative guesses about the 'real' number of 'illegal immigrants'. Also the last line of this paragraph again refers to 'huge numbers', an obvious ***hyperbole*** when it later turns out in the article that these numbers barely reach a dozen. In sum, the typical number game of immigration reporting has one main semantic objective: to associate immigration with problems and threats, if only by quantity. This is also why in the examples of raids being mentioned after this paragraph all numbers are printed in **_bold capitals_**, thus emphasizing again these numbers.

Note also the unexpected use of **_quotation marks_** for the word 'illegals' in sentence 2b. One might interpret this as taking distance from the use of 'illegals' in the rest of the report, as we do ourselves in this article, but no further evidence exists in the article that the authors take such distance. Therefore the quotation marks should be read as being used to mark the use of the adjective 'illegal' as a noun, and as short for 'illegal immigrants'. Note incidentally, that in sentence 2d another word is being used instead of 'illegal', namely 'unlawful', which also confirms breaking the law, but less harshly so than 'illegal'. In the following examples of raids, all those described as being arrested are repeatedly characterized as 'illegals'.

There is another element of empathy creeping into the article when the authors describe the immigrants as 'slaving'. This totally converts (and subverts) the earlier characterization of the immigrants as active and evil, and not as victims. This use might continue the **_thematic line_** of empathy, set with the earlier use of 'desperate'. On the other hand, the use of 'slave' presupposes 'slaveholders', and instead of mere empathy, this may suggest an accusation of restaurant owners who exploit their 'illegal' workers [...].

A numbered description of the raids carried out by immigration officers follows. These examples are being described as 'cases', as in a scholarly or clinical report. This use of **_jargon_** suggests objectivity and reliability: the _Sun_ has concrete evidence. In the next paragraph the _Sun_ even claims to have a scoop when it revealed 'exclusively' the previous day 'how an illegal immigrant was nabbed' in the kitchen of one establishment.

[...]

3   The battle to hunt down the furtive workforce is carried out by a squad of just 115 immigration officers.

As is well known for news, and as suggested above, **_numbers_** are the **_rhetorical_** device to suggest precision and objectivity, and hence credibility. Also in this report, we not only find the usual number game to count 'illegal' immigrants, but also other aspects of the operation by the authorities, which in the next paragraph is said to be carried out by a 'squad of just 115 officers'. And in the next paragraph it is said that an 'extra 40 men' more are planned to be drafted.

[...]

Results of the analysis

Our analysis has shown that reporting on ethnic affairs typically shows the following properties within the overall strategy of positive self-presentation and negative other-presentation:

- Immigrants are stereotypically represented as breaking the norms and the law, that is, as being different, deviant and a threat to Us.
- *We* as a group or nation are represented as victims, or as taking vigorous action (by immigration officials or the police) against such deviance.
- Such representations may be enhanced by hyperboles and metaphors.
- Credibility and facticity of reports are rhetorically enhanced by the frequent use of numbers and statistics.

Reading source

van Dijk, 2000, pp.42–8   ■ ■ ■

Van Dijk makes use of a number of terms to help analyse media language. These include the following, which I have formed into rough groups:

- *rhetoric, hyperbole, metaphor* and *rhetorical repetition* – these are terms referring to the persuasive function of language;
- *passive sentences, comment, topicalisation* – these are terms about the way in which language is structured, and about how (through this structuring) priorities are assigned;
- *register, lexicalisation, ingroup designator* – these are terms about the selection of words, with a particular selection having a particular persuasive function.

Van Dijk uses a variety of other words too: association, implication, capital letters, quotation marks, number game, thematic line, jargon.

BRITAIN INVADED BY AN ARMY OF ILLEGALS

Sun NEWS SPECIAL

By JOHN KAY and ALISON BOWYER

BRITAIN is being swamped by a tide of illegal immigrants so desperate for a job that they will work for a pittance in our restaurants, cafes and nightclubs.

Immigration officers are being overwhelmed by work. Last year, 2,191 "illegals" were nabbed and sent back home. But there are tens of thousands more, slaving behind bars, cleaning hotel rooms and working in kitchens. And when officers swoop on an establishment, they often find huge numbers of unlawful workers being employed.

CASE ONE: Last month officers raided the Casey Jones burger bar at Waterloo Station in London. TEN of the staff were carted off.

CASE TWO: In May, 1987, immigration officials swooped on London's swanky Hilton Hotel in Park Lane in a 2am raid, after a tip that one of the cleaners was working there illegally. They ended up taking away THIRTEEN Nigerians, all employed illegally.

CASE THREE: In Tenby in Dyfed, West Wales, police arrested the chef of the Golden Curry Indian restaurant last May. Unfortunately, they forgot to tell the diners. Customers were still waiting for their meals two hours later.

Furtive

The battle to hunt down the furtive workforce is carried out by a squad of just 115 immigration officers.

Yesterday The Sun revealed exclusively how an illegal immigrant was nabbed in the kitchen of Deals, the restaurant in Chelsea, West London, run by the Queen's nephew, Viscount Linley.

And now the Home Office have announced they are planning to draft in an extra 40 men to track down more.

Illegals sneak in by:
● DECEIVING immigration officers when they are quizzed at airports.
● DISAPPEARING after their entry visas run out.
● FORGING work permits and other documents.
● RUNNING away from immigrant detention centres.

They have little difficulty finding jobs, especially in London, because unscrupulous employers know that they can pay rock-bottom wages.

Cash

And they are invariably paid in cash with not a word to the taxman.

In West End restaurants and hotels employers often pay just £60 a week for 60 hours work.

But £100 a week to a Thai or Filipino is 10 times what they would earn in their homeland.

In 1987, officers nabbed

HOW THE ILLEGALS TOTAL HAS SHOT UP

HILTON . . . 13 workers were "illegals"

CASEY JONES . . . ten staff were carted off

DEALS . . . swoop on Viscount Linley's kitchen

2,191 illegal immigrants, a 39 per cent increase on the previous year.

Nearly 1,500 went back to their native countries voluntarily and 233 were deported. Most had lied their way into Britain.

Every year eight million foreigners from outside the Common Market enter Britain.

It is impossible for immigration officers to weed out all the would-be illegal immigrants. And once they are here, it is a nightmare trying to keep track of them.

Deport

The illegal immigrant employed at Lord Linley's restaurant was a Thai who had overstayed his visa by 12 YEARS.

Compared with most "illegals" he was paid well, £3.50 an hour plus a share of the tips.

He is not being deported because he has lived for so long away from Thailand.

Most of the illegal immigrants working in London are from the Far East and South America.

Back street "sweatshop" factories also use illegal immigrants to churn out cut-price goods.

They are also hired as servants and domestic helps in private homes.

An immigration officer says: "It is impossible to know how many illegal immigrants there are. "But we are certainly

stepping up our efforts to track them down."

It is difficult for the restaurant trade to work out who is a legal worker and who is not.

Francois Gijzels, managing director of The Hard Rock Cafe, one of London's trendy restaurants, says: "If the applicant isn't from the EEC we check their passport and they must have a valid work permit.

"I'd say one in 20 people who come here aren't entitled to work in Britain, so we show them the door."

Cash in hand makes it easy

BOSSES at the Rock Garden restaurant in London's trendy Covent Garden are strict about new staff but have still been tricked by false credentials.

Managing director Arthur Wickson says: "We check for passports, work permits and national insurance numbers, but have been caught out.

"Some illegal immigrants are a lot smarter than they look and have wised up on ways to obtain false identities and fake NI numbers.

"An Egyptian working for us as a waiter a few years ago convinced us he was legitimate.

Simple

"We had to sack him and it was only when he took us to court for unfair dismissal that everyone found out he had a false name, false passport—the works.

"Illegal immigrants make up a big part of Britain's restaurant staff, especially in London, and it is made simple for them by owners paying them cash in hand.

"We insist staff go on our payroll and work for a week before being paid."

'So many it is not possible to check'

Figure 4.1 *The news story analysed by van Dijk (see Reading 4.2)*

Many of the terms may be familiar to you from everyday usage. An *hyperbole* is a deliberate exaggeration. The idea that words have *associations* or *implications* is commonplace. Some words might be a little trickier. *Rhetoric* is the use of language to persuade or influence.

A *metaphor* is a figure of speech in which a word or phrase is applied to people, objects or actions to imply some kind of resemblance: the illegal immigrants are, in *The Sun*'s language, like an army.

Some terms used by van Dijk are more technical and their specific meaning here may not be in even a good dictionary. *Lexicalisation* refers to choice of vocabulary: the decision to use the term 'illegals' rather than other terms such as immigrants or migrants. *Register* refers to language associated with a particular social situation or subject matter: so army and invasion are both taken from a military register. A *passive sentence* is one in which the subject of the sentence (the person or thing 'doing' the action) is turned into the 'recipient' of that action: 'Britain invaded by an army of illegals' as opposed to the 'active' sentence 'An army of illegals invades Britain'. *Topics* and *comments* are key linguistic terms. The topic is the thing being talked about, the comment is the thing being said about it. In many languages, including English, sentences often follow a topic–comment structure. Britain is topicalised throughout the article by placing it first in sentences. Through being placed first in this way, Britain is turned into the point of focus, whereas the 'invasion' by the 'illegals' is turned into the comment. These choices of *syntax* (sentence structure) emphasise the supposed danger to Britain. Finally, the term *ingroup designator* simply refers to words that indicate membership of some kind of 'us' group, as opposed to 'them'. Do not worry if you have not grasped all these terms straight away. We will draw upon some of them on the DVD-ROM and practise their use.

The main point to take from this reading is that, as in the earlier reading from Norman Fairclough, the very close and precise attention to language in this analysis is used to generate broader results, in this case about the difference between positive self-presentation and negative other-presentation. Whereas Fairclough analyses a set of relationships created by texts (such as between the presenter and the audience, or between the vigilantes and the audience), the main relationship dealt with by van Dijk is 'us' versus 'them' – an 'us', which is construed as people who have not experienced immigration, whether legal or illegal; and a 'them' who are a threat to that 'us'. But both Fairclough and van Dijk use close analysis of language to dig out the latent or hidden meanings that lurk beneath media texts. This is at the core of what critical discourse analysis does. It is only by addressing broader questions concerning patterns of global migration and of ethnic inequality – a task that van Dijk undertakes elsewhere in the piece from which this reading is taken – that we can make connections between these individual examples of media texts on the one hand and broader patterns of power on the other. Effective critical discourse analysis always involves some social analysis.

3 Content analysis

We have seen how critical discourse analysis can help us to unpack the meanings of specific linguistic items in media texts (this can be combined with the analysis of visual elements) and to relate these meanings to broader sociocultural processes. But it is at this point that we need to confront the question raised at the start of the chapter. How can we generalise from these studies of specific texts to make arguments about, say, representations of vigilantes and/or crime on television during a particular period, or about representations of immigration in the press as a whole, rather than just in *The Sun*, one particular daily newspaper on one day? This is where content analysis can make a very important contribution. As with critical discourse analysis, the best way to demonstrate its potential usefulness is to refer to specific studies.

3.1 Race and poverty in the USA

Let us begin with a study by political scientist Martin Gilens (1996) of the way in which poverty was represented in the USA's leading news magazines (*Time*, *Newsweek* and *US News and World Report*) over a five-year period (1988–1992). As with Fairclough's and van Dijk's analysis, discussed above, while the specific study is relatively old, the issues raised remain current, as levels of inequality and poverty have risen considerably in the USA in recent years.

The following key figures were produced by Gilens:

- Gilens found 182 stories concerning poverty in these magazines during the period under analysis.
- 635 people were pictured as 'poor' in these stories, in 214 pictures (photographs and drawings).
- Gilens's interest was primarily in the representation of poverty in terms of 'race' and ethnicity. He excluded 75 people in eight stories whose race could not be identified; 635 minus 75 left 560 people pictured.
- Gilens found that of those 560 people pictured in news stories as 'poor', 62 per cent were African-American (see Table 4.1).

Why does this matter? Because, according to US government statistics, African-Americans in fact make up only 29 per cent of the US poor and this in turn is important because, as Gilens puts it:

> A reader of these news magazines is likely to develop the impression that America's poor are predominantly black [...]. This distorted portrait of the American poor cannot help but reinforce negative stereotypes of blacks as mired in poverty and contribute to the belief that poverty is primarily a 'black problem'.
>
> Gilens, 1996, p.521

Table 4.1 Stories on poverty in US news magazines, 1988–1992

	Number of stories	Number of pictures	Number of poor people pictured[a]	Percent African-American[b]
Time	44	36	86	65
Newsweek	82	103	294	66
US News and World Report	56	67	180	53
Total	182	206	560	62

[a] Excludes 75 people for whom race could not be determined.

[b] Difference in percentage African-American across the three magazines is significant at $p < .02$

Source: Gilens, 1996, p.521

So Gilens is dealing with a double problem surrounding US media representation: of the poor and of the African-American poor. However, Gilens goes further in his study than an analysis of this 'over-representation' of African-Americans as poor. He also shows that the major US news magazines also misrepresented other aspects of poverty, notably the age distribution of the poor, and the work status of the poor.

Regarding the first, age distribution of the poor, drawing on survey research, Gilens shows that the US public is much more sympathetic to children and older people among the poor than towards working-age adults. Gilens found that the news magazines were accurate in showing large numbers of children among the poor; and in showing that a large proportion of poor African-Americans were children (52 per cent in the pictures analysed, compared with 47 per cent in the census data). However, this accuracy is unlikely to affect public policy, claims Gilens, because 'sympathy toward poor children is often not translated into support for government aid when providing that aid means helping their working-age parents. In terms of public policy, therefore, the elderly are the only unambiguously privileged age-group among the poor' (Gilens, 1996, p.522). Yet while people aged over 64 account for 11 per cent of all poor people, they are almost invisible in magazine poverty stories (two per cent of the images – a total of just 13 people). The elderly account for eight per cent of all poor African-Americans, a slightly lower proportion than among the non-African-American poor, only two people. Yet only two of the 13 elderly people pictured as poor were African-American.

Regarding the second area of news magazine misrepresentation of the poor, their work status, Gilens puts the problem in the following way:

> For centuries, Americans have distinguished between the 'deserving poor', who are trying to make it on their own, and the 'undeserving poor', who are lazy, shiftless, or drunken and prefer to live off the generosity of others. ... More remarkable than the tenacity of this distinction is the tendency to place a majority of the poor in the 'undeserving' category. In one survey, for example, 57 per cent of the respondents agreed that 'most poor people these days would rather take assistance from the government than make it on their own through hard work'.
>
> Gilens, 1996, p.523

In fact, says Gilens, the census data show that most poor people of working age do work, at least part-time. But the poor, as represented in the major US news magazines, are much less likely to be employed than their real-life counterparts (see Table 4.2). Only 15 per cent of the sample of images depicted working-age poor people as working. What about African-Americans? The census data show that poor African-Americans are only a little less likely to work than the non-African-American poor – 42 per cent as opposed to 54 per cent. But the difference in magazine representations is much greater. Only 12 per cent of poor African-Americans of working age are shown in the magazines as working; whereas the figure for poor non-African-Americans in the magazines is 27 per cent.

Activity 4.1

Stop for a moment and make sure that you understand these figures. Do they matter? What do they suggest about representations of African-Americans in US news magazines? ■ ■ ■

I hope you will be able to see that poor non-African-Americans are shown as half as likely to work as they really are (27 per cent in the magazines, as opposed to 54 per cent in the census data); and that poor African-Americans are shown as three and a half times less likely to work than they really are (12 per cent in the magazines, as opposed to 42 per cent in the census data). In my view, what comes across very clearly and importantly in this study is that, even in highly professional US news magazines, patterns of representation reproduce stereotypes of poor African-Americans as lazy. This is almost certainly unintentional; but whether intended or not, it seems likely that such representations, in such influential magazines, will contribute to the reinforcement of such stereotypes among readers.

Table 4.2 Work status of the working-age US poor and work status of the working age 'magazine poor' by race (per cent)

	Total[a]	African-American	Non-African-American
True poor			
Working	51	42	54
Not working	49	58	46
Magazine poor			
Working	15[b]	12[b]	27[b]
Not working	85[b]	88[b]	73[b]
Number of working-age magazine poor	351	165	129

Significance levels indicate differences between magazine portrayals and census figures for each category. Working age includes those 18–64 years old.

[a] Includes 57 working-age poor for whom race could not be determined.

[b] $p<.001$

Source: Gilens, 1996, p.524

You can see from this summary of Gilens that content analysis can generate interesting *accounts* of media representation, involving potentially important *claims*. These accounts and claims can in turn contribute to larger *arguments* and *theories* about the media. But how is such content analysis carried out? And how effective and credible are the accounts and claims it produces? As we shall see, the two questions are very closely related. Good content analysis involves thinking carefully about how the research is being carried out – that is, about *methods*.

4   Criteria for evaluating accounts of the media

There are many different ways in which researchers think about the evaluation of claims and accounts about the media. One potentially useful way of approaching this issue is as follows: an effective claim or account concerning the media combines theory and evidence in a way that is *coherent, comprehensive* and *empirically adequate*.

■   *Coherence* concerns whether an account makes sense. This is partly dependent upon the clarity of the key claims and concepts in the argument, and this in turn will depend partly on the quality of writing. But it also involves the reasoning that links those concepts. Conclusions need to follow logically from prior arguments. Assessing this involves evaluating the plausibility and accuracy of the unspoken assumptions behind the claims, concepts and reasoning (see Goldblatt, 2000, p.145).

■ *Comprehensiveness* refers to the extent to which a claim about or account of the media successfully covers the range of theory and evidence relevant to the issue under discussion (Goldblatt, 2000, p.149). No account can cover everything, but we need to think carefully about the level of generality of evidence being used. Does the account rely on too narrow a range of instances, such as the experience of a particular society or section of a society? This is particularly important when it comes to evaluating theories of the media as a whole.

■ *Empirical adequacy* refers to the success or otherwise of an account of the media in using evidence and theory in such a manner that it justifies its conclusions. Does the evidence support the account?

It is important to understand that these three criteria are closely interrelated. For example, an empirically adequate account involves using evidence that is sufficiently comprehensive for the account to be coherent.

Considering media research methods, both in textual analysis and beyond, involves thinking about empirical adequacy. An effective use of a media research method is one that produces empirical evidence that adequately supports effective claims and accounts about the media and their place in the social world. As we shall see, those who favour quantitative methods and those who favour qualitative methods tend to have different understandings of what constitutes an effective claim or account. To explore this further, and to examine the procedures by which content analysis might produce such adequate evidence – in other words, to think about how to do content analysis – let us return to Martin Gilens's account of representations of poverty and race in US news magazines.

4.1 Doing content analysis effectively

Content analysis can be said to involve four main stages (see Figure 4.2):

1   Formulating a *problem* or question.
2   Deciding on the range and size of a *sample*.
3   *Counting* within that sample, and *coding* the data.
4   *Interpreting* (and writing up) the data.

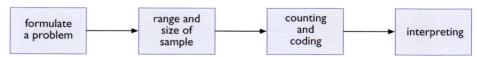

Figure 4.2 *The four main stages of content analysis*

Gilens began with a *problem*. According to survey research, the US public substantially exaggerates the percentage of African-Americans among the poor. This not only reinforces negative stereotypes, it also leads to a situation in which many white people do not support government welfare provision because they perceive poverty and/or unemployment as a 'black problem' (you might recognise parallels in your own country). So Gilens decided to investigate media representations of poverty and race, on the basis that skewing of information in media texts might be responsible for the skewed understanding of the situation on the part of the US public. In order to carry out this investigation, Gilens would have had to have made decisions about his *sample*, including decisions about what range of media output to consider. In theory, he could have analysed a much wider range of representations than the news magazines he ultimately came to study. He might have drawn on major US newspapers, television news stories, documentaries, advertisements, and so on. This would certainly have helped Gilens to draw more general conclusions about the representation of race and poverty across different US news media – thus potentially adding to the comprehensiveness of his account. But content analysis is time-consuming, and such a wide sample may well have been impractical. Moreover, if Gilens had gone for samples from a wide range of media, assuming he had a limited amount of time and resources, he would have had to have used smaller samples in each of the media studied. By choosing to focus on one very influential medium, the major news magazines, Gilens was more easily able to extend his initial sample to 214 images than if he had tried to study a number of different media. Other things being equal, the larger the sample, the greater is the likelihood that patterns detected in an analysis are not the result of accident. Gilens may well have opted to choose a bigger sample in one medium, rather than a number of smaller samples in a range of media.

There may have been another factor behind the decision to focus on one medium. By concentrating in detail on one medium, Gilens was also able to extend his analysis over time, to five years. Supposing that there had been a major news story in one year concerning poverty, perhaps, say, as a result of a government report on black poverty? This may have led the news magazines to feature more poor black people than usual, and this would have exaggerated the results. By comparing results across five years, Gilens was able to show that there were no major differences across this period in the representations he detected. These are decisions about empirical adequacy in terms of *generalisability*, which have important implications for the comprehensiveness of Gilens's account. He may have lost generalisability in terms of the news media as a whole by choosing to include only magazines, but he gained it in terms of the specific medium he chose to concentrate on, namely the news magazine.

Integral to these decisions about the size and range of the sample would have been a wider decision, informed by reading and research in the area, about how to examine representations of race and poverty within news magazines. Gilens could, for example, have found every story about African-Americans in the news magazines and analysed how they talked about poverty. In fact, he decided to concentrate only on those stories that were 'primarily focused on some aspect of poverty or poor relief' (Gilens, 1996, p.519). This might have meant that he missed smaller references to poverty in other stories about African-Americans. But this decision would mean that he was able to cover a larger number of stories specifically on poverty (again, assuming a limited amount of time and resources to carry out the research). Moreover, as Gilens points out, 'to the extent that stories that focus on African-Americans also discuss poverty, the body of stories examined here will *underestimate* the true degree to which poverty is presented as a black problem' (p.519, emphasis added). This means that a sceptical reader could not validly claim that Gilens was subtly exaggerating the problem through counting spurious items.

Activity 4.2

Gilens's next major decision would probably have been about *counting*: specifically, *what to* count. Stop and think for a moment. If you were carrying out a similar content analysis of news magazine stories about poverty, in terms of the degree to which poverty was associated with a particular 'race', what would you count? Would it be the language used about black and white poor people, or the images of them? ■ ■ ■

There is no right or wrong answer to Activity 4.2. Gilens might have analysed words or images. If analysing words, he might have concentrated only on headlines or only on lengthy stories, in order to keep the amount of work down to an achievable level. In fact, after an initial identification of stories based on the written text, the analysis was made of the *images* accompanying such stories. Counting words as well as images may well have been helpful, but the images alone were probably enough to make an important initial point about representation. As we have seen, 214 pictures – the vast majority of them photographs – containing 635 poor people, were found accompanying the 182 stories on poverty.

'Counting' in content analysis involves *coding* the data. This means coming up with relevant categories and assigning the data to categories. Because Gilens's research problem was well defined, these categories/codes would have been relatively easy to find. There were three initial codes: black, non-black, or not determinable. Seventy-five images of people were assigned to the last category, leaving a working sample of

560 images of people (the initial 635, minus the 75 not determinable). But as we have seen, Gilens and his assistants also coded the images for whether the people were depicted as working or not; and according to age. The reasons for this were given earlier: Gilens provided evidence to suggest that these issues strongly affect public perceptions of the 'worthiness' of the poor, affecting public attitudes, and ultimately policy, towards welfare and poverty. Coding might also have been carried out for sex, able-bodiedness, and so on, but Gilens's interest was such that he decided not to pursue this route.

Such coding raises another issue, which is important to empirical adequacy: *reliability*. As one writer puts it, 'an important aspect of reliability concerns the degree of consistency with which instances are assigned to the same category by different observers or by the same observer on different occasions' (Hammersley, 1992, p.67). The racial status of the people in the pictures may have been ambiguous; the coder may have had her or his own distinctive view of what constituted 'black' or 'non-black' or 'elderly'. To make sure such potential problems did not distort the empirical adequacy of his results, Gilens assigned a random 25 per cent sample of the 214 pictures to another coder. There was almost complete agreement between the two coders, indicating that the initial coding was highly reliable. But while race might be relatively unambiguous, what about age, which Gilens also analyses? Gilens assures us that in coding for age, 'a very lax criterion was applied, so that any poor person who could at all plausibly be thought to be over 64 years old was so coded' (Gilens, 1996, p.522) and, as with race, a test for intercoder reliability was carried out.

4.2 Conflicting research traditions: positivism and interpretivism/constructionism

I have concentrated in some detail on Gilens's research, which is only one of thousands of pieces of content analysis research that have been carried out on the media, in order to demonstrate the procedure behind effective content analysis and to explain what might constitute empirical adequacy in this context. As we have seen, this involves questions of generalisability and reliability. It also fundamentally involves the notion of *validity*: the aim is to achieve as truthful or accurate an account as possible of the phenomenon being studied, even if we can never be entirely certain whether an account is true (Hammersley, 1992, p.69).

However, at this stage it is important to register that not all media researchers would see our criteria of coherence, comprehensiveness and empirical adequacy in quite the same way. Two opposing philosophical traditions are often said to underlie social and cultural research, including media research: the positivist tradition and the interpretivist or constructionist tradition (the following account draws on Redman, 2005). In brief, the positivist tradition believes that investigating the social world is not significantly different from analysing the natural world, and that social science should follow natural science in a number of ways:

- by observing and precisely measuring the phenomenon under study;
- by seeking to remain detached from the object of study and thereby avoiding the confusion of facts with values;
- by identifying causal explanations that can serve as the basis for generating universal laws.

By contrast, those drawn to the interpretative or constructionist tradition instead tend to be more concerned with exploring the way in which people make sense of their social world, rather than to establish claims about cause and effect, or to create generalisable knowledge. There are 'strong' and 'weak' versions of this tradition (see Redman, 2005), but there is a tendency at the stronger end to see truth and reality as socially constructed, whereas positivists would tend to see them as independently existing phenomena that research can uncover. In fact, the term 'positivist' is often used as a crudely dismissive term, and few researchers would now call themselves positivist. Indeed many researchers would not wish to label themselves by either term. It is best to think of these as tendencies in research. (Significantly, the distinction between positivism and interpretivism in social science is related to another split, that between realism and constructionism, outlined in Chapter 5. Suffice to say that the differences at stake in both cases are part of a larger series of arguments over how we make sense of the world in the contemporary period.)

Many (but by no means all) researchers using qualitative research methods – including discourse analysts – tend towards the interpretative/constructionist tradition. Many (but by no means all) researchers using quantitative research methods – including content analysis – show the influence of positivist concerns. Both would be concerned with coherence, comprehensiveness and empirical adequacy, but interpretative/constructionist researchers would see themselves as making *more limited claims* than those working within the positivist tradition. The 'strong' interpretative tradition would tend to see knowledge, in the words of Stephanie Taylor, as 'situated', meaning that 'claims which are made can refer only to the specific circumstances of place, time and participants in which the research was conducted' (Taylor, 2001, p.319). I explained at the beginning of this chapter that content analysis is more concerned with generalisability than is discourse analysis. You may be able to see from Taylor's words why discourse analysts and those tending towards the interpretivist/constructionist tradition are less concerned with generalisability as a way of achieving empirical adequacy than are those quantitative researchers carrying out content analysis.

An important consequence of these differences of approach for studies of the media has been a division of labour. Many researchers work exclusively on either quantitative or qualitative methods, and this has a further, unfortunate consequence: it is rare to find studies that combine the two methods. However, in the next section, I want to show that quantitative and qualitative methods *can* be combined, by exploring how content and discourse analysis might be used to investigate different facets of the same problem.

5 Combining content and discourse analysis: families on talk shows

The problem I want to investigate is the way in which the institution of the family is represented on contemporary daytime talk shows on UK television. By 'talk shows' here, I mean the kind of 'reality TV' or 'problem' talk show of which *Trisha* (which ran on ITV from 1998 to 2004 and then on Five from 2004 onwards as *Trisha Goddard*, see Figure 4.3) is a leading example, where people in difficult situations appear on the show, rather than celebrities, as is the case with the conventional 'chat show'. I can only hint at how this might be done, as a full combination of content and discourse analysis would use up far more space than I have available. But let us begin with a discourse analysis.

5.1 A discourse analysis of *Trisha*

In the episode of the talk show *Trisha*, broadcast on ITV on 4 October 2004, host Trisha Goddard is interviewing three people from the same family for a section of the programme called 'I want you to divorce my daughter'. Philip and Leanne are a couple with a four-year-old daughter, who live next door to Leanne's mother Susan. Susan is interviewed, and complains about Philip's behaviour and about the rows between Philip and her daughter. Philip then enters and he and Susan start to shout at each other. Leanne comes on and tells them to stop arguing. There is further discussion of who is wrong and who is right. Two members of the audience give their opinion. The first accuses Susan of not being a sufficiently loving mother, eliciting a furious response from Susan. The second tells Philip to grow up, and instructs Leanne to leave her mother and find a decent husband.

Figure 4.3 *Trisha Goddard on the set of her daytime talk show,* Trisha Goddard

At this stage, Trisha intervenes. A transcript is provided below.

Trisha	Philip, without Leanne, what would your life be?
Philip	Nowt.
Trisha	Who keeps you on the straight and narrow?
Philip	Leanne.
Trisha [to Leanne]	Do you feel you do?
Leanne	Yeah.
Trisha [to both]	Do you want to be together?
Philip and Leanne	Yeah.
Trisha	So if you do move away from Susan, you're not going to be moving on from your problems. You're going to have to deal with them ... on your own. Now there's already a trust issue. [to Leanne] Do you think that Philip is still cheating?
Leanne	No.
Trisha	You think he's only cheated those three times?
Leanne	Yeah.
Trisha	Are you willing to forgive him for those three times?
Leanne	Yeah.
Trisha	You are. OK, it's your decision.

Leanne	I know I'm stupid. I know, I am stupid. But it's what I want and I have told him [Trisha: mmm] I have put my foot down.
Trisha	What happens if you he cheats on you again? Is there an ultimatum there?
Leanne	That's it, I've told him, I've said 'if it happens again, that's it, it's over, there's no turning back'. He knows all that.
Trisha	I think that sounds fair enough. [to Philip]Have you had a family while you're growing up yourself?
Philip	I've been in foster care.
Trisha	Can I just say to you: physical abuse is one thing but if you're having arguments next door, i.e., [to Leanne] your Mum can hear what's going on, then what is happening to your little girl, who is … how old?
Leanne and Philip	Four.
Trisha	What is she hearing under her own roof?
Leanne	And she's taking it all in.
Trisha	She is taking it all in. [To Philip] You know what it's like to have people you love mess with your head. You need to remember that, *right now*. You are doing in a different way what you feel was done to you. You are messing with her head. That argument, there's the shouting between the two people that she loves, will give her a tough time, and you know what that is like.
Philip	Yeah.
Trisha	You have no right to dish that on to another generation. So what I'm saying, even if you do move away, and I suggest [to Leanne's mother Susan] that Susan, you being against them, has actually kept them together even longer than they might have been in the first place, but [to Leanne] if you do move away, never mind about proving to your Mum that you can get on, you need to prove to that little girl, so she can be a healthy child. You know what I mean healthy? Not just body, this as well ['this' isn't shown but we can assume Trisha indicates her head]. Because sure enough if you don't she will be back on this show when she's a teenager with all kinds of problems. Do whatever

> you need to do, be it counselling, family therapy, but get it fixed, and get it fixed *fast*. [audience applause and cheering]

First of all, let us examine the extract using critical discourse analysis.

Activity 4.3

Fairclough's categories of representation, identities and relations might be usefully applied here.

- What *identities* are set up for those involved in the programme? You might want to think about this in terms of class, gender and ethnicity.
- What *relationships* are established between the different people involved (host, guests, the live audience, the audience at home)?
- How is the modern family being *represented* here? ▪ ▪ ▪

One dimension that might be brought out by a discourse analysis concerns gender. The segment constructs Susan and Leanne as two women struggling to be good mothers, whose efforts are constantly thwarted by a feckless man, Philip (whose time in prison and sexual infidelity are emphasised even before the credits of the programme). Another concerns class: a UK audience could not fail to recognise the accents, clothing and speech as those of a working-class family. Trisha meanwhile is presented as an expert professional. A third set of identities, around race and ethnicity, are very complex. Here is a black presenter exerting authority over a white family. Given the genre, Trisha's blackness – black presenters remain a rarity on UK television – evokes the doyenne of such talk shows, Oprah Winfrey, whose blackness, in the US context, strongly connotes an ability to understand suffering and marginalisation (some of the reasons behind this are made clear in the Gilens article, discussed above).

As for the *relationships* set up between the participants, the most striking feature for me is the absolute authority of Trisha over her guests and over the audience. All is chaos and conflict until Trisha intervenes to restore order with her homily on the need to protect the innocent – a conclusion that no-one could argue with. Cue frenetic applause. An important feature of this intervention is Trisha's invocation to Leanne and Philip to undertake counselling or family therapy. This advice is given in what initially appears to be an open way – 'do whatever you need to do', but in fact the only options seem to be either counselling or therapy. And the relationship that Trisha establishes with her guests is like that between a certain kind of counsellor and her clients: she allows the family to speak, she asks questions, and then she delivers a judgement that combines understanding with firm advice.

These identities and relationships result in a particular *representation* of the family. Talking to professional experts, and receiving their counsel, is presented as the way in which working-class families might mend their broken lives. So at one level, Trisha *represents* the world as a place of family conflict and trauma, which can be mitigated by emotional talk, guided by professional experts. Yet there is something more to the programme's representation of the world which works against this notion of expertly guided talk as a mitigation of trauma, and produces an ambivalent latent meaning in the text: the show, like other talk shows of its kind, has a carnival atmosphere, where audience members openly sneer at guests, and attack them for their negligence or stupidity. As in Fairclough's *This Week* example, information and entertainment are in tension, and Trisha's advice is so basic (don't argue in front of the children, go and see a professional counsellor) that it is hard to see how the programme would really inform anyone about how to deal with a difficult family situation of the kind on display here. But this helps to produce the ambivalence: it is as if Trisha cannot quite resolve away the nastiness of the world in spite of the applause. And this is affirmed by our knowledge, backed up by frequent reminders of what is coming up next, that there will always be more (working-class) guests, with more problems, in the next segment, in the next episode(s).

5.2 A possible content analysis of talk shows

Assuming that my qualitative discourse-analysis account above is reasonably coherent and empirically adequate, let us now look at how it might work *together* with some quantitative content analysis. One fruitful way in which the two might be combined is that discourse analysis can be used to generate claims, the comprehensiveness of which can be tested using content analysis. Another is that discourse analysis's ability to uncover latent meanings can complement content analysis's ability to focus on manifest meanings (see Section 1 of this chapter). Let us examine these issues now.

Activity 4.4

What claims about the representation of the family might we derive from the discourse analysis above?

1   That the episode of *Trisha* represents the working-class family as a place of trauma, which can best be aided by professional experts, but with strong limits on that aid?

2   That *Trisha* (the programme as a whole, not just this episode) represents the working-class family in this way?

3   That the daytime 'problem' talk-show genre on UK television represents the working-class family in this way?

4   That UK television represents the working-class family in this way?   ■ ■ ■

Perhaps you will agree that, without further research, only the first of the four statements in Activity 4.4 could really be derived from this discourse analysis. In other words, the empirical evidence produced by the discourse analysis can not be used to support broader claims about media representations of families. There are limits to the comprehensiveness of our account, but as long as we are only making limited claims, that might be all right: the evidence might be considered adequate to support a limited, but coherent, account. The second claim could only be adequately supported by more research on other episodes of *Trisha*. In order to be reasonably sure about (3), we would need to carry out analysis across a range of other programmes within the genre. Claim (4) would be much more challenging, because this is such a broad question that it would be difficult to answer it at all without a vast sample – and discourse analysis can only deal in very small samples, because it involves the intensive study of particular moments.

So content analysis could complement our discourse analysis by extending the comprehensiveness of our account to (2) and, preferably, to (3). This might allow us to say something of significance about a particular genre and its representations of family and class. Claim (4) would almost certainly be too large even for content analysis – but remember that if we did some coherent and empirically adequate content analysis on one particular genre, others might be able to apply our tools to other genres, such as soaps and situation comedies, to build a broader account of television representations of working-class families.

We might proceed in something like the following way. Using magazine listings and video recording (we might well need research funding to help with this task), we could record every daytime talk show broadcast on UK terrestrial television in a particular month. As daytime talk shows are divided into multiple segments, we could then list all the segments. This would be our sample. My estimate is that this would come to about 240 segments (four main shows of this genre currently on UK terrestrial television, five days for each of four weeks in a month, about three segments per show). This is our sample (stage 2 of a content analysis – see Section 4.1 above). But what to count and how to code it (stage 3)? We would need something that would not require detailed analysis of each segment, otherwise the analysis would be just too time-consuming. We could limit the issues to 'how many of these segments are about working-class families in conflict and/or trauma?' and 'in how many segments is counselling or therapy mentioned as a possible solution?' Coding would then involve attributing segments to these categories, or not. At the end of this, we would have two sets of statistics. Also, by keeping a record, we could observe whether this percentage varies differently across the different talk shows, which would further help us in our genre analysis.

Of course there would be significant challenges. We would need to establish some principles for judging: who was middle class and who was working class when it came to coding the people on the screen; what would constitute conflict and trauma; and what the criteria are for interpreting a recommendation of counselling. These are questions of reliability (see Section 4.2 above). If we follow Gilens's careful procedures, we would ask a second coder to check a certain number of our segments to see whether she or he agreed with the first coder's categorisations. If there was a low level of agreement, then we would have a problem of empirical adequacy. Then we would have to be careful about how to interpret the results in a valid way, so that our empirical evidence adequately supported our account (stage 4).

But if such challenges were successfully negotiated, we might well be able to argue that a key contemporary genre, watched by millions of people every day, consistently shows working-class families engaged in conflict, and that therapy and counselling are consistently offered as solutions. Discourse analysis may help with this by helping us to produce an adequate set of assumptions about what constitutes trauma or conflict. But more significantly still, discourse analysis would complement these claims about the talk-show genre by examining a different kind of meaning. Here it is important to recall the distinction I made at the beginning of this chapter, between latent and manifest meaning. The content analysis deals with relatively manifest or clear meanings, rather than latent ones: the appeal to counselling in the *Trisha* extract can be said to be pretty obvious, rather than subtle and concealed. But it would be much harder for a content analysis to get at more complex issues of meaning; for example, regarding the *ambivalence* of the programme about such counselling discourses. This is where discourse analysis can really be useful. The analyst (in this case, me; in earlier cases, Fairclough and van Dijk) brings to the surface meanings that might not be obvious even to regular viewers. Because the two methods deal with such different types of media meaning, combining them might be really fruitful for an analysis of the daytime talk show as a whole, and might lead on to further work on other genres and even other media.

When combining these two methods, we still need to consider questions of coherence, comprehensiveness and empirical adequacy. A vital part of producing a coherent, comprehensive and empirically adequate account of representations of working-class families in daytime talk shows would be to consider what claims we *could not* make. Neither the discourse nor the content analysis could be used in themselves as the basis of claims about the impact of such programmes on their audiences. This would need to be explored via some form of audience research (see **Gillespie, 2005**). Nor could these methods of textual analysis tell us how and why these programmes come to take the form that they do. For this, production research, linked to more general sociocultural analysis, would be necessary (see **Hesmondhalgh, 2006**). But the combination of discourse and content analysis might well produce a fairly coherent, comprehensive and empirically adequate account of the representation of family and class in these texts; and further work on production and on audiences could build upon this.

6 Conclusion

This chapter has compared content analysis and discourse analysis as methods of textual analysis. As I explained at the beginning of the chapter, the reason for considering them together here is that they represent two contrasting types of research: the quantitative and the qualitative. Discourse analysis involves the close interpretation of (mainly) language; content analysis involves the counting and measuring of items, including words and images. The former is better at analysing latent meaning, the latter is better at dealing with manifest meaning. I then proceeded to show how discourse analysis can work, using linguistics-based critical discourse studies by Fairclough and van Dijk. Content analysis was introduced by referring to Martin Gilens's study of representations of poverty and 'race' in US news magazines. I then raised the key question of how research produced by these (or other) methods might be evaluated – Section 4 introduced us to three criteria: coherence, comprehensiveness and empirical adequacy. To explore what might constitute empirical adequacy in content analysis, and to outline the way in which researchers carry out content analysis, we examined issues of generalisability and reliability in relation to Gilens's account. However, I cautioned that two different traditions, the positivist and the interpretative/constructionist, would approach these criteria somewhat differently; and explained that many (not all) quantitative researchers tend more towards positivist understandings, and many (not all) qualitative researchers tend towards interpretivist/constructionist understandings. I explained that this has helped lead to a division of labour in media research, in which quantitative and qualitative methods are rarely combined. Using a combination of discourse and content analysis to explore representations of family and class in daytime talk shows, Section 5 argued that such a combination could in principle be fruitful if careful attention was paid to questions of coherence, comprehensiveness and empirical adequacy. So, it seems possible to conclude that discourse and content analysis are both potentially fertile methods for examining issues of media and power. They might prove to be even more productive when brought together.

DVD-ROM

Now that you have finished reading Chapter 4, work through the Discourse and Content Analysis activities in the Chapter Activities area of the DVD-ROM, *Analysing Media Texts*. ■ ■ ■

Further reading

Bell, A. and Garrett, P. (eds) (1998) *Approaches to Media Discourse*, Oxford, Blackwell. A collection of a variety of different forms of discourse analysis, including Fairclough and van Dijk, focusing mainly on news.

Benton, T. and Craib, I. (2001) *Philosophy of Social Science*, Basingstoke, Palgrave. An excellent account of debates about positivism and its critics.

Deacon, D., Pickering, M., Golding, P. and Murdock, G. (1999) *Researching Communications*, London, Arnold. An excellent book on media research methods, including discussion of the positivist and interpretative traditions, and of discourse and content analysis.

Entman, R.M. and Rojecki, A. (2000) *The Black Image in the White Mind: Media and Race in America*, Chicago, IL, University of Chicago Press. Impressive content analyses of many different aspects of media representations of ethnicity.

Fairclough, N. (2003) *Analysing Discourse*, London, Routledge. This is not specifically about media texts, but it is a coherent and comprehensive theorisation of the place of textual analysis in social research.

Philo, G. and Berry, M. (2004) *Bad News from Israel*, London, Pluto. Philo is a leading member of the Glasgow University Media Group, whose content analyses have provided important and controversial contributions to debates about the media for three decades.

van Dijk, T.A. (1991) *Racism and the Press*, London, Routledge. A very thorough and convincing study of racism in the UK press, using critical discourse analysis.

References

Evans, J. (2005) 'Celebrity, media and history' in Evans, J. and Hesmondhalgh, D. (eds) *Understanding Media: Inside Celebrity*, Maidenhead, Open University Press/The Open University (Book 1 in this series).

Fairclough, N. (1995) *Media Discourse*, London, Arnold.

Foucault, M. (1977) *Discipline and Punish*, London, Tavistock.

Gilens, M. (1996) 'Race and poverty in America: public misperceptions and the American news media', *The Public Opinion Quarterly*, vol.60, no.4, pp.515–41.

Gillespie, M. (ed.) (2005) *Media Audiences*, Maidenhead, Open University Press/The Open University (Book 2 in this series).

Goldblatt, D. (2000) 'Living in the after-life: knowledge and social change' in Goldblatt, D. (ed.) *Knowledge and the Social Sciences: Theory, Method, Practice*, London, Routledge/The Open University.

Hammersley, M. (1992) *What's Wrong with Ethnography: Methodological Explorations*, London, Routledge.

Hesmondhalgh, D. (ed.) (2006) *Media Production*, Maidenhead, Open University Press/The Open University (Book 3 in this series).

Redman, P. (2005) 'In search of authoritative sociological knowledge' in Redman, P., Silva, E.B. and Watson, S. (eds) *The Uses of Sociology*, Milton Keynes, The Open University.

Taylor, S. (2001) 'Evaluating and applying discourse analytical research' in Wetherell, M., Taylor, S. and Yates, S.J. (eds) *Discourse as Data: A Guide for Analysis*, London, Sage/The Open University.

Titscher, S., Meyer, M., Wodak, R. and Vetter, E. (2000) *Methods of Text and Discourse Analysis*, London, Sage.

Van Dijk, T. (2000) 'New(s) racism: a discourse analytical approach' in Cottle, S. (ed.) *Ethnic Minorities and the Media: Changing Cultural Boundaries*, Buckingham, Open University Press.

The politics of representation

Jason Toynbee

Contents

Chapter 5

1 Introduction

The first three chapters of this book have dealt with particular aspects of the way in which texts 'work'. Semiotic, narrative and genre analysis each offer a means of understanding *how* texts produce meaning. These approaches also enable us to tackle the question of *what* is meant by texts, particularly in relation to the three key themes of power; change and continuity; and knowledge, values and beliefs. To use the language of semiotics from Chapter 1, we might say that Chapters 1 to 3 outline ways of analysing the process of signifying, in order to help us establish what might be signified. Chapter 4 does this too, but its emphasis is rather different, in that it suggests that important questions about the reality of what is signified may arise from inconsistencies within media discourse, or from quantifiable deviations between media accounts of the world and the world itself.

In the present chapter we follow up the broad issues emerging here, namely the status of media texts in relation to the world, and the possibility of realism. The debate is between two approaches, according to which texts either:

1   construct the images, identities and understandings of the world that pervade our lives, or,

2   show a pre-existing, real world beyond that of the text itself.

These are called, respectively, constructionist and realist approaches to textual analysis. They diverge strongly in that the first begins from the premise that our world is largely a mediated world, which is not just accessed through symbolic structures such as language and genre, but is actually produced by them. For instance, in considering television news as melodrama (Chapter 2), or through examining its narrative organisation (Chapter 3), we are being invited to take a constructionist position. It is suggested that news programmes do not so much report events in the world, as provide stories of what the world is like. These have the flow and controlled release of knowledge typical of a soap opera. What is more, as with a soap, the news offers emotional release – countless opportunities for identifying with fellow humans who have struggled, suffered or found joy in their lives. Just as in 'fictional' media texts, what counts is how the news as a symbolic package not only delivers pleasure and meaning, but also produces the world as we know it.

Conversely, the realist approach holds that objects and events exist beyond texts and independently of them. From this perspective the news is, or should be, an account of what is happening, a means of finding out about the world. That 'should be' is important. A key problem which any realist analysis of media has to confront is how to establish what might be the truth. This is not so much because of the physical difficulties in gathering information that media producers might have; arguably, new media technologies, from the microphone to the satellite camera, make this easier. Rather, the issue bears on the way in which reality is contested, the way in which there seems to be conflict over what exactly is occurring in the social and material world. As I write (in 2005), a war of occupation rages in Iraq. Immediately, though, I have to stop. Is it a *war* that is *raging* (which is my sense of things), or are we instead confronted by the resistance of insurgents to a legitimate government supported by its freedom-loving allies, which is the way the situation in Iraq is framed by some news programmes? This example of two conflicting ways of representing a set of events suggests that power relations will strongly influence what is claimed as real in media texts. This means that, while both realist and constructionist analyses of media texts are concerned with signifying practices (connotation, narrative, genre, discourse, and so on), there is going to be a big difference in goals. Realists will be concerned with the problematic relationship between texts and reality: not only with how texts might reveal that reality, but also with the ways in which they may systematically distort or cover it up in the interests of power. This kind of approach to texts, where falsification of the truth is at stake, is often called ideological critique. It has been a major tradition in media studies and I will have more to say about it shortly.

The goal of constructionist analysis, on the other hand, is to show how meaning and world view radiate from the text. For constructionists there is a potentially endless chain of signifying. Jostein Gripsrud, calling on the work of C.S. Peirce, refers to this in Chapter 1 as 'unlimited semiosis'. He gives the following example: 'The sign "sun" may for instance be interpreted, associated with or perceived as "star", a radically more distant and possibly extinguished sun. The new object will then be "a star (in the sky)". The term "star", the new interpretant, may then by some be taken to mean "movie star" – and a series of new interpretants is then made possible' (see Chapter 1, Section 5).

In other words, the transformation of the meaning of 'star' is a semiotic or, in the terms I am using here, a textual process. The emphasis is on how new meanings emerge within the world of the text and are then disseminated through what we might call the text of the world. The transferred meaning of 'star' enables 'starring', 'stardom' and, in turn, the everyday phrase 'you're a star'. This is a textbook case of construction in which new meanings and values derive from the realm of the symbolic.

Realists, by contrast, would seek an explanation for the transformation of meaning outside the text. What in the social world, they might ask, has led to the signifying reach of a particular word being extended to well-known film actors? One explanation could be that 'stars' are granted mythical powers as a way of distracting attention from the powerlessness experienced by ordinary people in their everyday lives. Stars, and the film-texts in which they are presented, are thus thoroughly ideological. (For varying perspectives on these issues see **Evans and Hesmondhalgh, 2005.**)

Perhaps it is now starting to become apparent why this chapter is entitled 'The politics of representation'. The two ways of approaching media texts that have been introduced each have strong political implications. Most realists work from the position that we do not live in the best of all possible worlds, but rather an imperfect and unequal one. From this perspective texts consist of symptoms or reflections of such a world, including the aspirations of the people who live in it, for a better life. Conversely, when constructionists pose the question of power it is in terms of a symbolic relation – power as enacted through the text itself. It follows that politics will be conducted at the level of the text. For instance, the genre of melodrama might be said to provide a virtual space of empowerment in which the everyday world of women is transformed. Another example: in the 1970s African-Americans re-imagined themselves as strong and glamorous through 'blaxploitation' movies such as *Shaft* (USA, dir. Parks, 1971), rejecting the handed-down identities of the 'good negro' or the 'laughing minstrel' that had previously circulated through the media. One implication here is that politics in the constructionist approach are generally redemptive; texts can change our understandings of ourselves, and so transform lived experience.

I have sketched out some ways in which this chapter deals with power, and with continuity and change (a critical view of the reflection of entrenched political power in the news; a more optimistic take on the construction of changing identities in film). But what about knowledge, values and belief, the other theme foregrounded in this book? In an important sense this chapter is concerned with this theme at every point, for the argument between realists and constructionists is at the core a dispute about the nature of knowledge and its attendant concepts, values and belief. To put it simply, where realists have a two-stage model (1, the world; 2, how we know it), for constructionists, knowledge is produced in and through symbols – there is only one level.

Over the course of this chapter, I will follow up these issues by tracing key debates and by looking at some short case studies of textual analysis that bring the question of the politics of representation to the fore. The first section outlines a series of arguments concerning the nature and potential of realism, made from within a broadly realist position. In the second section I examine the problem of ideology, and assess the argument that media texts misrepresent reality in the interests of power. Interestingly, in much of the critique of ideology it is apparently realist texts (Hollywood films, for example) that are the most ideological because they are the most capable of convincing us, through their implicit claim to be realistic.

Finally, in the third section we examine constructionism. This is the last of the three positions to develop in media studies outlined in this chapter. It follows logically from the critique of ideology in that media texts are held to have a world-shaping effect. The difference is that external reality now disappears. As we have just seen, in this view, media and reality are more or less on the same plane.

2 Probing realism

Much everyday criticism of media texts is realist. People tend to make judgements based on how far a film, programme or story is true to life. Generally the more real the events depicted appear to be, the better. In an obvious sense this applies to factual genres like the news because they *claim* to report actual events in the world; less obviously it is also true of fiction. Yet some of the key arguments about realism have dealt with fictional genres: the fact that fiction makes no claim to present actual events begs important questions about the status of the reality that it is supposed to reveal. For this reason we will be discussing fiction (see Chapter 4 for issues of realism in relation to factual genres).

If a realist take on the media is deeply embedded in contemporary culture it would be wrong to assume that this is natural or inevitable. Rather, like all tendencies in culture, realism is a historical phenomenon. We can identify two main aspects to it: an artistic approach (which has been more or less consciously adopted by artists and other symbol makers), and a series of arguments about what it is that realism consists in, deployed by critics. As we will see, these have sometimes run together: a playwright such as Bertholt Brecht was simultaneously a writer, a director and a critical theorist of realism.

2.1 Realism: a selective history

The representational arts of painting and literature have always been concerned with imitating life in some sense. However, in the early nineteenth century, with developments in European painting and the novel, symbol makers began to adopt explicitly realist goals and reflect on the question of what techniques and themes might best serve the purpose of depicting reality. Moreover, in the relatively short period since, there has been a proliferation of different kinds of realism, as well as arguments about its nature. Realism has kept on changing.

What key themes might we pull out of this history? Firstly, it is fair to say that realist texts have been concerned with portraying ways of life and, to a greater or lesser extent, the social organisation that underpins them. This has often involved looking across social divisions, focusing on the working class as well as on the more privileged sections of society, which had been the subject of most earlier art. Secondly, realist texts have attempted to show a psychological reality; their aim is to reveal how individuals think and feel. For Georg Lukács (the Hungarian critic of the realist novel), writing in the mid-twentieth century, it is the connection between these different emphases which is key. As a Marxist he is interested in how novels can show the nature of life under capitalism through individual characters, and the situations in which these characters interact. Such characters and situations he calls 'types'.

Reading 5.1 Activity

Lukács suggests how the type offers a means for the novelist to confront a split in the way life is understood in 'modern bourgeois society'. Read the following extract from Lukács' *Studies in European Realism* (Reading 5.1), and consider what is the nature of that split.

Reading 5.1

Georg Lukács, 'Studies in European realism'

[T]he live portrayal of the complete human personality is possible only if the writer attempts to create types. The point in question is the organic, indissoluble connection between man as a private individual and man as a social being, as a member of a community. We know that this is the most difficult question of modern literature today and has been so ever since modern bourgeois society came into being. On the surface the two seem to be sharply divided and the appearance of the autonomous, independent existence of the individual is all the more pronounced, the more completely modern bourgeois society is developed. It seems as if the inner life, genuine 'private' life, were proceeding according to its own autonomous laws and as if its fulfilments and tragedies were growing ever more independent of the surrounding social environment. [...]

[...]

The true great realists [...] knew that this distortion of objective reality (although, of course, due to social causes), this division of the complete human personality into a public and a private sector, was a mutilation of the essence of man. Hence they protested not only as painters of reality, but also as humanists, against this fiction of capitalist society however unavoidable this spontaneously formed superficial appearance. [...]

Reading source
Lukács, 1972/1950, pp.8–9 ■ ■ ■

For Lukács there has been a false separation of life under capitalism into public and private (or social and individual) spheres. However, he does not think that the 'type' as represented in the novel provides a simple solution for this dichotomy; the type is in no way a stereotype. Rather, in typical characters and situations, the novelist must show the complex interrelation of social relations and the psychology of the individual in a particular historical situation. In so doing, Lukács asserts, the very best realist writers may achieve a view of the 'totality', that sense of the interconnectedness of everything, which is in danger of disappearing as modern societies become more fragmented and more divided into public and private realms.

It seems, then, that the realist project is a difficult one. Yet for this very reason Lukács is hard on novelists who fail to rise to the challenge that he sets out. Chief among these is the French 'naturalist' Emile Zola, many of whose books are about working-class life at the end of the nineteenth century. As well as the focus on working-class experience and struggle, there is extraordinary attention to detail. His novel *Germinal* (Zola, 1998/1885), for example, depicts the people and industrial landscape of north-eastern France in a careful, almost microscopic fashion. It might therefore seem surprising that the Marxist Lukács is so critical of Zola but the thrust of Lukács's criticism is that, in striving to accurately portray the social world, Zola ends up producing 'reportage', or mere description. The underlying structure of power relations is thereby obscured. It is actually in the more bourgeois settings of the realist novels by Balzac, Dickens and Tolstoy that we find typical characters and situations that reveal the totality of life under capitalism.

Lukács's powerfully argued theory has provided something of a point of departure for arguments about realism. Indeed, his approach was closely scrutinised quite early on, in a debate he had with fellow Marxist writers during the 1930s (Adorno et al., 1980). The contribution of one in particular is important. The German playwright Bertholt Brecht objected that the novels which Lukács champions deal mainly with the lives of the bourgeoisie, the prosperous middle class. The working class is therefore excluded, and this absence is damning. Furthermore, Lukács remains backward-looking in his admiration for the classic realist novel. Both the nature of the capitalist world and the form of art have changed since the nineteenth century. As Brecht puts it: 'Methods become exhausted; stimuli no longer work. New problems appear and demand new methods. Reality changes; in order to represent it modes of representation must also change' (Adorno et al., 1980, p.82).

Brecht is defending his own practice as a playwright here. He uses avant-garde techniques such as bizarre make-up, discontinuous jumps from dramatic scene to declaimed chorus, and the mixing of film with live performance in order to expose a system – capitalism – that produces poverty, mass unemployment and dictatorship. (By the time he wrote the passage quoted above, Brecht was living in Denmark, as an exile from Hitler's Nazi regime.) Brecht's reasoning is that the working-class audiences he wants to reach need to be shocked into seeing things for what they are; yet at the same time they must be brought into the theatre and entertained. To try to achieve this he adopts characters and devices from popular culture – songs, gangsters, comedy, pirates, the quick costume change.

We will return to Brecht's radical approach to realism later on, but we ought to finish this section by looking at an example of the way in which a more orthodox, social realism has been incorporated into the mass media. In parallel with the intense theoretical debate about the form of the realist text during the twentieth century, a more pragmatic approach was being developed by many writers and directors. British cinema provides a case in point.

In the mid-1950s there had been a sub-genre, the 'social problem film', which dealt with the lives of working-class people. Some of the films in this cycle are fairly stilted and patronising. In *I Believe in You* (UK, dir. Dearden, 1952) two probation officers, one of whom (Henry Phipps) has just retired from the colonial service, steer a couple of juvenile delinquents out of trouble and, at the end of the film, into marriage (see Figure 5.1).

Figure 5.1 *A still from* I Believe in You *in which Phipps (an upper-class probation officer) talks to his young charge, Hooker. The streets of post-Second World War London are shown behind them*
Source: Canal+ image UK Ltd

Two aspects of working-class life emerge in particular. One is its otherness. As Phipps walks into the streets of south London, a voiceover gives his response. Here are 'places I'd never heard of, never knew existed'. This, of course, is the position with which we are invited to identify: that of the comfortable middle classes for whom working-class districts are profoundly alien. Secondly, working-class people are presented as child-like and susceptible to 'bad influences'. The two probation officers are in effect surrogate parents, in a situation where real parents either wash their hands of the young or over-cosset them.

Such an approach changes dramatically with the arrival of 'British New Wave' cinema at the end of the 1950s. Now, perhaps for the first time in British films, there is a 'commitment to a politically serious representation of working-class experience' (Hill, 1986, p.1). What has changed? Firstly, and most obviously, the films are shot on location, chiefly in the towns of northern England, so that there is constant observation of everyday life just as in the naturalist novel (see Figure 5.2). This is a world where the domestic is dominated by the industrial, and where kitchens, and the little terraced houses which contain them, are pressed in on all sides by grimy mills, factories and railways.

Figure 5.2 *A still from* A Kind of Loving. *The two central characters, Vic and Ingrid, are shown with the industrial landscape of northern England in the background*
Source: Canal+ image UK Ltd

Secondly, *all* of the characters tend to be working class, and it is therefore an ostensibly working-class point of view which is being offered to us. This aspect demonstrates the influence of the Italian 'neo-realist' cinema of 10 years earlier. But where the Italian films (for example, *The Bicycle Thieves* (Italy, dir. De Sica, 1948) and *Bellissima* (Italy, dir. Visconti, 1951) had portrayed the essential dignity of the poor, the emphasis in British social realism is on alienation and dissatisfaction. In *A Kind of Loving* (UK, dir. Schlesinger, 1962), which is set in a Yorkshire town, smart Vic gets dull but pretty Ingrid pregnant and then marries her. Even before the wedding, however, he feels trapped and, after she loses the baby, he leaves. Vic does come back to Ingrid after a while yet at the end of the film we are left without any sense of things having improved. Vic's thwarted ambition and sexual frustration, and Ingrid's limited imagination, remain deeply embedded.

What are we to make of these so-called 'kitchen sink' films? On the one hand we have seen how they might be said to represent an advance on the preceding social problem films. There is closer examination not only of place, but also of people and their relationships. On the other hand this very focus ultimately undermines realism, in the sense of explaining how society is structured. As John Hill puts it '[c]lass is presented as primarily an individual, rather than collective, experience, a moral, rather than socially and economically structured, condition. As with the social problem film, the stress is on the inter-personal drama rather than the play of social and political forces' (Hill, 1986, p.57).

Hill's criticism, somewhat reminiscent of Lukács, suggests that realism in popular cinema is elusive. The more human interest there is, the enactment of love, hate, hope and disappointment on an individual basis, the more difficult it is to show structural inequality and its ravages. In effect, the concentration on the personal hides those *im*personal social forces that do so much to shape people's lives.

Whatever their limitations social–realist films of the New Wave have had a profound influence on British media culture, feeding a strand of film-making and television drama that has persisted in the period since. We can turn now to a television situation comedy, *The Royle Family* (UK, BBC2, 1998–2000), which encapsulates both continuity and change in this tradition. Yet our interest here is not really in the Britishness of the programme so much as in its 'mode of representation', to use Brecht's term. That is to say, we are concerned with *how* it attempts to represent reality. There may well be lessons from this case study that we can carry across to other realist texts.

Study note *You can view clips from* The Royle Family *in the Viewing Room area of the DVD-ROM,* Analysing Media Texts. *You might find it useful to have a look now at clip 4 and think about the ways in which this could be considered a social–realist piece and, more generally, how far comic genres can be realistic.*

2.2 Case study: realism and *The Royle Family*

The situation of *The Royle Family* is that of a northern English working-class family consisting of father (Jim), mother (Barbara), daughter (Denise) and son (Anthony). Denise's boyfriend (Dave) and Barbara's mother (Norma) also make frequent appearances. Members of a family next door (the Carrolls) turn up from time to time as well. The setting is the Royles' home, with most scenes being staged in the living room, as the family sit watching television and talking. One further point needs to be made. Each half-hour episode takes place in 'real time'. In other words, there is no narrative ellipsis or temporal cutting within episodes, and each weekly episode is purported to be in a successive diagetic week (see Chapter 3 for a discussion of narrative and time). In this way our time lived as audience members is apparently synchronised with the time of the narrative.

We can start by examining the unusual temporal structure. Most importantly, it is an attempt to represent the everyday, repetitive and banal nature of the life of the Royles, and of working-class life more generally (see Figure 5.3). We see this in the very first episode, when Barbara is on the phone to her mother. All around her the family is slumped, in immobility and torpor, watching the television.

Barbara's 'It's all go here', as she begins the conversation with Nana, comically emphasises the fact that it is *not* all go in the Royle living-room. In effect Barbara establishes the terms and conditions of the situation: nothing happens in the house, or nothing of conventional narrative significance. For in contrast to an orthodox sitcom, where in each episode one or more characters attempt to change the status quo only to be frustrated at the end, in *The Royle Family* the characters acquiesce with their situation.

As a result narrative development is minimal, and what there is tends to be distributed through the series. In the first episode Barbara gets a job; Jim's birthday is in episode four; while the whole first series has as a continuous story line during the six-week build-up to Denise's wedding, which is in the final episode. Much of the comedy then derives from this 'thinning' of narrative and, with it, the constant repetition of certain cameos. One example is Barbara's question to visitors about what they have 'had to eat for their tea'. More than a running gag, this is a narrative device which points up daily banality. In sum, it seems that the characters are funny in *The Royle Family* precisely because they do not try to transcend their situation, but are instead immersed in it.

Figure 5.3 *Members of* The Royle Family *in a typical pose; a close-up of the banality of everyday life*
Source: BBC

If *The Royle Family* is low in event, it is high in texture. The fabric of relatively impoverished working-class life is observed with an almost obsessive gaze. Episodes often begin with a shot of ordinary things – a bare foot with painted, but chipped, toe nails, a plate of half-eaten dinner, or a birthday card depicting a golfer. The dominant shot, however, is of the whole living room relayed from a static camera set at about the same height as, and to one side of, the television. This dwells on the recumbent characters as they stare at the television. There seems to be a double borrowing here. In part such camera work is reminiscent of the British New Wave with its lingering shots of static figures in kitchens, or industrial landscapes. But it is also possible to detect the influence of the television 'fly on the wall' documentary, where close-ups of domestic interiors abound.

In *The Royle Family* the camera has a set of particularly favoured objects. To begin with there is the human body and its functions. We watch and listen to constant ingestion – of food, cigarette smoke and drink (both tea and alcohol). This is matched by the continuous emission of farts, belches and occasionally tears. In most episodes Jim announces he is going for a 'tom tit' (rhyming slang for 'shit'), and accordingly leaves the room. In addition to the body and what it takes in or puts out, the other class of object that looms large is the domestic artefact, often shown in extreme close up: crockery, pots and pans, the television and, most obsessively, the living room ashtray – large, made of pink glass and always overflowing with stubs. Now on one reading (reading one) this seems dangerously close to mockery. Are we not being invited to laugh *at* the Royles, their home and the stereotypical behaviour in which they indulge? These people are the *un*worthy poor: lazy, vulgar, ignorant and dishonest (see Chapter 4, Section 3.1 for a discussion of the discourse of the unworthy poor).

However, if this reading is available then so is a much more critical, realist interpretation – arguably one towards which the text is pushing us. On such a reading (reading two), *The Royle Family* is not only about the Royles and their way of life; the programme also plays with a set of expectations concerning the portrayal of the working class, and even manages to comment on modes of realism found in the media. Firstly, we *can* identify to some extent with the characters and their extraordinary talent for getting by. Where in reading one the Royles are ignoble, in reading two they have a certain dignity. True, Jim is mean and has disgusting personal habits; undoubtedly Denise is spoilt and self-indulgent; and young Anthony is picked on in every episode. But ultimately these people get along. The family is a functional one which cares. Its members are interested in each other.

Secondly, Jim's view of things (represented by his bitter jokes, and even his meanness), invites a comic recognition of the limitations and frustrations of working-class life: the trap of unemployment, the constant need to watch pennies and the inability to put one's talents to productive use. Significantly, Jim's jibes are often at the expense of Barbara or her mother, Norma. The two older women in the family are constantly the objects of laughter. They almost never make jokes themselves, but are funny because of their 'natural' stupidity and a propensity to victimhood. Jim, and to some extent, Denise and Dave, at least have a comic knowledge of the nature of their entrapment, a partial class-consciousness. Barbara and Norma, on the other hand, have very little knowledge, and what they do know is either absurdly superficial or beside the point.

Yet by the same token it is Barbara and Norma who most often bear witness to the inequality of working-class life. During Barbara's telephone conversation with Norma in episode one, we learn that the older woman has tried to use an out-of-date discount voucher for 20p. At first sight this is absurd – 20p seems a triflingly small sum; yet it bears witness to a central fact of her existence – poverty. Another example is when Barbara learns that Dave's mother has bought a wedding outfit from Marks and Spencer (an upmarket shop): her wistful sigh, 'Marks's eh?', is a poignant marker of material deprivation. Such moments are not dwelt on in the programme, but they do nonetheless raise the issue of the barbarity of the class system for a second or two.

Thirdly, there is a constant problematisation of realism itself. As we read earlier, in Section 2.1, John Hill (1986) criticises the 'kitchen sink' films because social class can only be seen through the thick mist of inter-personal relations. Certainly that is true of *The Royle Family*. Yet there is also a distancing effect which keeps us from identifying too closely with the drama of personality and relationship. There are two aspects to this. One is that reading one (giving a negative view of the Royles) is constantly available, and occasionally pushes its way forward – Jim really is lazy and disgusting, Barbara is stupid, Denise selfish. The result is ambivalence. We see the negative class stereotype even as we gain a more positive insight into working-class life. This reduces audience identification with the characters, without eliminating it completely. The other aspect of this distancing effect is to do with genre and the dual sitcom/documentary mode of the programme. The blemished skin and mascara revealed through lingering close-ups and the ashtray with 27 cigarette stubs; these pieces of highly personal reality are scrutinised in a close, documentary fashion. Yet, because we are watching a sitcom, we do not expect such intrusiveness. The result is slight shock or discomfort.

To a limited degree, then, *The Royle Family* produces something like that alienation effect which Brecht advocated in the 1930s. A gap is opened up between text and audience, a gap that provokes thinking and engagement with the world being represented, and which may even hint at the systematic unfairness of society. We should not make too big a claim here, however, for, if *The Royle Family* is mildly critical, it also celebrates how people can cope with the little they have got. Indeed, as we have seen in this section, much of the comedy focuses on strategies for 'getting by'. This blunts the programme's critical edge.

In Section 2, I started by examining debates about realism, and then explored some of their implications through the case study of *The Royle Family*. Perhaps the main points to draw out are that, for those critics and producers who are committed to it, realism should not simply reproduce the appearance of things but attempt to reveal the structure of society, or at least some of the forces which shape it. However, this is a difficult goal, mainly because the means of representation so often seem to get in the way. Sometimes the drama of human interest obscures social comment, and sometimes conventional story telling reduces its impact.

The result is that one particular strand of realist texts and criticism
(it might be called Brechtian) has increasingly reflected on representation
itself. In order to show *what* is real the focus has shifted, in part at least,
to *how* the real might be portrayed. We have seen something of this in
The Royle Family.

What causes these problems of representation? Why is it so difficult
for media texts to show social reality? It is these questions that
ideological analysis of media texts has tried to answer, and it is to that
approach we now turn.

3   Ideological analysis

A general definition of ideology might be 'a set of ideas or beliefs'.
However, the concept of ideology that has been taken up in the social
sciences and humanities has a more specific meaning, one strongly
influenced by the approach of Karl Marx. His writings on the subject are
few and scattered but provide a foundation, which others have built on.
Here is an extract from one of them:

> The ideas of the ruling class are in every epoch the ruling ideas, i.e.
> the class which is the ruling material force of society, is at the same
> time its ruling intellectual force. The class which has the means of
> material production at its disposal, has control at the same time over
> the means of mental production.
>
> Marx, 2004/1932

We can see here Marx's emphasis on the role of ideas in sustaining the
power of the ruling class. In capitalism this class is the bourgeoisie, who
own 'material production' – the factories or, more generally, the economy.
Ideology is, then, that set of ideas which encapsulates the power of the
bourgeoisie, making it seem right and natural. A key aspect of this is that
ideology misrepresents the class nature of society to those who are
exploited, namely the working class.

3.1 Ideology and film theory

Ideology became a key concept in social and media studies in the 1970s.
This was partly due to the social upheaval during the 1960s and 1970s.
In 1968 there had been waves of demonstrations and strikes across
western Europe and North America. It seemed to many that revolution
was imminent. Yet this revolution was never achieved and, during the
decade that followed, many young, radical academics wanted to find out
why. Ideology provided a powerful explanation. The great mass of people

were being systematically misled about the state of the world and prevented from seeing that their interests lay in changing it.

One theorist of ideology was particularly important at this critical moment. Louis Althusser (1971) followed Marx in understanding ideology as 'mental production', but went much further in the claims he made for its scale and power. Firstly, he suggested that ideology was all pervasive, stretching from common-sense ideas in everyday life through to theoretical reflection in the social sciences. Secondly, he argued that ideology was as much about being as knowing. The key work done by ideology was in summoning up that deep sense of subjectivity, the 'I', which we use to name ourselves. For analysts of film, first in France and then in the UK, this seemed an incredibly fruitful way of understanding how we engage with films. A film, on this view, addresses each spectator as an individual subject; it calls each watching 'I' of the audience into the world of the film so that each one suspends disbelief in the text's fictional nature (see Figure 5.4). What is more this happens unconsciously – it seems perfectly right and natural to 'enter into' films.

Figure 5.4 *For film theorists such as Baudry, the cinematic apparatus works by drawing the audience into identification with the on-screen image, summoning up a particular subjectivity, or sense of self*
Source: Getty Images

In an influential essay the French film theorist Jean-Louis Baudry (1992/1975) suggested that such a process was an effect of the 'cinematic apparatus'. By this he means the complete technical system from camera to screen, and including the spectator, whose role is to complete the circuit of meaning-making. For Baudry the camera is the 'eye of the subject'; it relays images to the spectator which always position her or him at the centre of things. Although constant shifts from shot to shot might be thought to disrupt this centring effect, Baudry argues that projection in the cinema restores continuity and unity. The spectator is magically granted the facility to make sense of shot-to-shot sequences on screen. In a similar way camera movement within film space boosts the mythical power of the spectating subject: one can apparently see everywhere. Finally, Baudry suggests that there are *two* levels of identification in the cinema: as well as identifying with the gaze of the camera (the higher or 'transcendental' level at which the subject is constituted), the spectator identifies with particular characters.

Activity 5.1

Go to the cinema or, if you are unable to fit this into your busy schedule right now, watch a film on video. As you are watching, consider Baudry's conception of the 'cinematic apparatus'. How far and in what ways is your own subjectivity and identification as a spectator determined by camera, editing and that restoration of continuity which is achieved on screen? ■■■

Baudry's is a very strong statement of the ideological effect of film, and you may find yourself resisting its implications – that you have neither control over your mental processes when you watch, nor any knowledge of this ideological effect. Still, Baudry is important in media studies because of the generality of his approach. He suggests a way in which all fiction films *systematically* produce a particular kind of spectating subject.

In the UK the application of Althusserian ideas took a rather different form. In another influential essay, Colin McCabe (1981/1974) argued that the 'classic realist text' (CRT) of the nineteenth century novel provides a model for understanding ideology in the fiction film. In the novel there is a 'hierarchy of discourses' whereby narrative prose (text which is not within quotation marks) has a special truth-telling function. It also organises, and grants or withholds authority to, the speech of characters (text which is within quotation marks). Crucially the narrative prose, or 'metalanguage', appears transparent, its status as discourse being hidden from the reader. When one reads narrative prose, one simply absorbs what is said without realising that it is *being said*. This is profoundly ideological, in that our engagement with the story is based on an illusion.

McCabe then applies the CRT model to the fiction film, using the example of the Hollywood murder mystery *Klute* (USA, dir. Pakula, 1971). He suggests that what the leading female character (a prostitute named Bree) says about herself, in the form of over-dubbed extracts from conversations with her psychiatrist, is of a lower truth-value than the images that we have of her actions. She does things which seem to contradict what she says. Conversely the discourse of the detective, John Klute, is highly authoritative. McCabe's point is that as a detective, concerned with finding things out, what Klute says and sees constitutes a 'discourse of knowledge'. What is more, 'it is as a full-blooded man that he can know not only the truth of the mystery but also the truth of the woman Bree' (McCabe, 1981/1974, p.220).

A number of points can be drawn from this. Firstly, with the transfer of the CRT model to the fiction film, the hierarchy of discourses now consists not only of different kinds of language but also includes knowledge that is relayed through the image. What the camera shows is as important as what people say. Here, in his attention to the visual, McCabe is quite close to Baudry. Secondly, in the case of *Klute*, the ideological effect of the hierarchy of discourses is to privilege *male* discourse. McCabe demonstrates how a man's view of the world, and of male power, is treated as 'natural' in the film. Crucially, because the spectating subject does not recognise the hierarchy of discourses, she or he fails to see the ideological process of naturalisation. This extension of ideological effects to include the representation of gender marks an important step in media studies. Increasingly it is not only class relations that are ideologically misrepresented, according to media text analysts, but also gendered power.

3.2 Ideology in practice

How far can we still use these approaches from the mid-1970s, with their arguments for extremely powerful ideological effects in film? In order to address this question let us examine the film melodrama *Imitation of Life* (USA, dir. Sirk, 1959). If you have not seen it, you can get a flavour of it from the clips on the accompanying DVD-ROM, *Analysing Media Texts*. The film concerns the consequences of a chance meeting between two women and their daughters. Annie Johnson is a maid who has been finding it hard to get work since she was abandoned by the father of her daughter, Sarah Jane. Lora Meredith is an aspiring actress who has been widowed, and now struggles to look after her daughter, Susie. After their initial meeting Lora takes Annie and Sarah Jane to live with her – Annie as maid. The narrative then tracks the four characters over 10 years or so. Key to the storyline is that Lora and Susie are white, Annie is black, while Sarah Jane looks, and can therefore 'pass' as, white.

What drives the narrative is really the struggle of the characters to achieve fulfilment in a hostile world. Lora wants to break into acting, Susie seeks her busy mother's love and attention, Sarah Jane yearns to escape from a black identity for which she is stigmatised, while Annie wants the best for Sarah Jane but cannot bear the fact that her daughter wants to leave both her mother and her ethnicity behind.

Now, on one level it could be argued that this is a deeply ideological film. What the film shows through its hierarchy of discourses is the *inevitability* of a social world ordered by racial and gendered power. Sarah Jane's struggle to escape black identity is rewarded with torment and degradation, and although Lora does achieve success as an actress, in the end she turns away from the theatre to marry Steve, the man who has faithfully stood by her since the beginning of the film. In the final shot, of the inside of a car as it moves slowly along in Annie's funeral cortège, Steve smiles as Lora embraces Susie and Sarah Jane. It is his look, the 'discourse of knowledge', which confirms that this is a moment of narrative closure: Lora has accepted her role as mother and wife, thus redeeming all the pain and suffering that the film has depicted.

Against this ideological reading, however, we have to note a series of contradictions. For one thing there is simply too much attention paid to Lora and her triumphant ascent as an actress for this to be a matter of straightforward disapproval. It is difficult not to see Lora's struggle to achieve success against all the odds as admirable. Equally, while the representation of racism seems to confirm it as a social fact, and although we are invited to admire Annie's fortitude in the face of inevitable adversity, there is also a strong sense that racial injustice is unbearable. At the end of the film it is revealed to Lora (and the audience) that Annie had been a respected community leader in the black church as well as being a faithful servant. That this should have been hidden is hardly tolerable, even within the 'inevitablist' discourse of the film as a whole.

Finally, the representation of Sarah Jane, and her trials and tribulations, is shot through with contradiction. She looks white, but 'is' black; and she suffers because of intolerance, yet is punished for trying to escape it. What is more, she is a powerfully sexual figure. It is as though, despite the appearance of whiteness, her racial identity returns through her overt sexuality. The discourse of the 'good and respectable Negro' is thereby undermined, even as yet another stereotypical discourse (black = sex) is inserted.

We can sum up, then, by saying that, while film theory can offer insights into ideology in *Imitation of Life*, in the end the ideology at stake here is too big and monolithic to explain the tensions running through the text. It is difficult to draw lessons from a single case, of course, but the general trend in film and media studies, away from the model of ideology presented in the 1970s, would certainly reinforce this impression. As later critics have observed, media texts rarely carry the full ideological load that writers like Baudry and McCabe proposed. There is often much more ambiguity or contradiction than they give credit for.

Another, related, point follows. With film theory's conception of ideology, reality has almost disappeared. As we saw earlier, according to Marx, ideology consists in those ideas which obscure or justify social relations of domination – the power of one group over another. Crucially, then, ideology is a form of illusion. For the writers influenced by Althusser, however, it is no longer seen as false knowledge because it is virtually everywhere. In practice, there is no thinking outside ideology. The point is pushed home in the criticism of realism. Realist texts are the most ideological, suggest the film theorists, precisely because they appear to be realistic. Such a move effectively removes the possibility of getting access to the real, certainly in fictional texts.

But does this have to be the case? Is an all-pervasive and all-powerful ideology the only model available? In the last part of this section we will examine some alternative positions, together with their consequences for textual analysis.

3.3 Cutting ideology down to size

One response is to rethink ideology, reducing the scale and scope of its effects so that it no longer pervades everything or founds our self-hood. Focusing on television rather than film, Stuart Hall (1997/1974) takes this route. Ideology is 'encoded' into texts, Hall suggests, but different audience groups are capable of 'decoding' texts in different ways. Some spectators will indeed acquiesce to the 'preferred meaning' of the text as it has been encoded. Others will make a 'negotiated' reading in which they accept some but not all of the preferred meaning. Still others will engage in an 'oppositional' reading, not only disagreeing with the preferred meaning, but also recognising its ideological nature and role in justifying power relations. Hall's approach makes ideology critique more flexible, and acknowledges the fact that not all audience members read texts in the same way. What is more, resistance to ideology, and thus access to the real, is possible. Indeed, from the perspective of the encoding–decoding model, the reading we have just done of *Imitation of Life* might be considered oppositional. It is an attempt to 'see through' the preferred meaning of the film.

Another approach has been to take into consideration the historical moment in which texts are made and received. As John Thompson puts it:

> symbolic forms [loosely meaning texts] or symbolic systems are not ideological in themselves: whether they are ideological, and the extent to which they are, depends on the ways in which they are used and understood in specific social contexts. ... This approach may lead us to regard a symbolic form or system as ideological in one context and as radical, subversive, contestatory in another.
>
> Thompson, 1990, p.8

With social and historical context kept in the foreground it becomes possible to understand why *Imitation of Life* is so contradictory a text. The film was produced in 1959, two years after troops were used to escort black children into a formerly whites-only school in Little Rock, Arkansas, USA. As a result of the campaign of the Civil Rights Movement in the southern states of the USA, the area with the most deeply entrenched racism, desegregation was just beginning to happen. But hard and bloody struggles by black people were still ahead. This was also the period of the Cold War. Among sections of the white population fear of the Soviet Union and Communism ran alongside fear of blacks and of their growing political confidence. Meanwhile white liberals were reflecting on what they should do in a society where overt racism was tolerated and even encouraged. These factors go some way towards explaining the uncertainty and ambivalence about race that we have identified in *Imitation of Life*. The 'inevitablist' discourse of racial domination is still in place. Yet it is starting to buckle under the weight of its own contradictions.

There is a cultural context to consider too. The late 1950s was a time when black American music was starting to cross over into the mainstream white market. As well as rock'n'roll, with its basis in rhythm and blues, black jazz and sacred music were now much more prominent. In a sense the USA was acknowledging the centrality of black culture to its identity even as large parts of the white population held grimly on to racial power. This contradiction is played out in the film. The title track, *Imitation of Life*, is performed by the black singer Earl Grant. His crooning vocal style, set against strings in the manner of the hugely successful cross-over artist Nat King Cole, connotes wistful sophistication. Throughout the film, strings (without vocals) are used in the more melodramatic scenes as a way of highlighting intense emotion. A continuity between, ostensibly, white orchestral music and black popular music is thus established. However, in the night club scenes unadorned jazz (both modern and pre-war styles) is used to accompany Sarah Jane's dancing. And, at the end of the film, we see the spiritual singer Mahalia Jackson performing the traditional sacred song *Trouble of the World* from the pulpit at Annie's funeral service, her face contorted with the grief of centuries of oppression. Music in *Imitation of Life* thus carries a range of discourses of blackness at this key moment in the struggle for emancipation.

It seems, then, that bringing historical and social context into play enables us to put ideology 'in its place'. More, it means that we can bring realism into the same frame as ideological critique. *Imitation of Life* can be classified as a melodrama (see Chapter 2) but it is also a social problem film, and its attempts to deal with questions of race and gender reveal a realist intention. That the film fails to grasp the deep structure of the social relations it depicts shows the power of ideology, but not its *total* power. Indeed, we can expect media texts to be more or less ideological according to the balance of political forces in a given historical moment. The contemporary period, we ought to emphasise, is a historical moment too.

We have been looking at one broad way of dealing with the problems of 'big ideology', namely to reduce its scope, recognise its limited effectiveness, and examine media texts in their historical context. However, another response is the move towards constructionism. Here, in effect, the scope of big ideology remains. What changes is the status of reality. For the Althusserians, knowledge of reality was always a theoretical possibility, even if theorists of ideology were the only ones capable of understanding it. But in much contemporary textual analysis there is no longer a separate reality to be perceived behind the appearance of things. Instead there is just appearance: the world is *constructed* through language, images and texts. What you see, read and think is what you get. This is a simple concept yet a difficult one to grasp because it cuts so strongly against common sense. We will examine it in more detail in the next section.

4   Constructionism and the media

Let us begin with semiotic theory. You will remember from Chapter 1, Section 2.1 that a key innovation in semiotics was the proposal that sign systems function in an arbitrary way. In language there is no necessary connection between a word (the signifier) and the concept attached to it (the signified). Rather, the relationship is established through convention. 'Cat' means a small furry domestic animal in English because that is what the rules of the English language specify. In French, on the other hand, a different signifier, 'chat', is used. A more radical proposal follows from this: convention depends on a structure of signification. 'Cat' means cat in English because it is not 'house' or 'mouse' or indeed a similar entity like 'kitten' or 'puss'. That is to say, the signifier 'cat' achieves its meaning through its difference from other signifiers. The whole thrust of semiotics, then, is that language does not reflect a world of pre-existing objects, but rather carves up the world into objects through its function of coding. People say 'cat', therefore cat exists.

This is a profoundly radical move, and one which upsets common-sense notions of how language works. Still, in media and cultural studies such a view has itself become something like common-sense, and its scope has been extended beyond language to include the production of meaning in all signifying systems. Consider photography. At first sight photographs hardly seem to be coded. The meaning of a photograph, unlike language, derives from the direct resemblance it bears to the people and things it depicts (see Chapter 1, Section 5.1 for another discussion of this). In one of his earliest essays on photography the semiologist and critic Roland Barthes (1977) wondered how this might be so. Here, it seemed, was 'a message without a code' (Bathes, p.17). The photographic image, in other words, was a direct copy of the real objects before the camera. Yet at the same time Barthes recognised that photographs have connotations. A single image can signify a complex range of qualities in what is depicted: 'joy tinged with sadness'; 'innocent young man' – the range of possible connotations is vast. Moreover, this coding of photographs is controlled through sophisticated techniques; for instance, a particular choice of shot or frame, the use of light and, of course, decisions made at the developing and printing stages. Other theorists (for example, John Tagg, 1988) have gone much further: it is the coding of photographs which defines their meaning, while the mere fact that a photograph is 'of' something is more or less insignificant.

Interestingly Barthes, the great pioneer of semiology, held on to a dual view of photography (its uncoded *and* coded nature) all his life. Nevertheless, his work has played a key role in media studies in the development of thorough-going constructionism and, associated with it, scepticism about the existence of the real beyond sign systems.

4.1 Media texts in postmodernism and after

There is, however, another tendency here which we need to examine. As we have seen, semiotics is based on the concept of structure, a structure of difference among signifiers. But an influential group of theorists, including Derrida, Lacan, Baudrillard and the later Barthes, has argued that the structure of signification is itself a myth. Meanings change, the signifier slides, and the text, which once appeared to be well ordered, is actually fragmented and eclectic – made up of many texts. When applied in media and cultural studies this approach has sometimes been described as 'postmodern'. It supposes not only that signification is fluid but also that this is becoming more and more the case. In a nutshell, postmodernism continues the constructionist thrust of semiotics, but suggests that what is constructed is an ever-changing network of meanings rather than a stable and homogeneous world-view.

The following extract from Jim Collins's essay, 'Television and postmodernism', represents such an approach. Collins is discussing a drama series from the late 1980s, *Twin Peaks* (US, ABC, 1990–1991). This seems in some ways to belong to the genre of murder mystery. But, as Collins suggests, its multiple references to other genres and its use of distinct 'tones' make this attribution difficult.

Reading 5.2 Activity

Read the following extract from Jim Collins, 'Television and postmodernism' (Reading 5.2), and consider these questions. What does Collins mean by 'parodic discourse' in the first paragraph; and what qualities might *non*-parodic discourse have? In the second paragraph, Collins talks about 'the "suspended" nature of viewer involvement in television'. Refer back to the discussion of Baudry's 'cinematic apparatus' in Section 3.1. What differences are there between Baudry and Collins concerning the way in which media texts involve, or position, spectating subjects?

Reading 5.2

Jim Collins, 'Television and postmodernism'

The style of *Twin Peaks* is aggressively eclectic, utilizing a number of visual, narrative, and thematic conventions from Gothic horror, science fiction, and the police procedural as well as the soap opera. This eclecticism is further intensified by the variable treatment each genre receives in particular scenes. At one moment, the conventions of a genre are taken 'seriously'; in another scene, they might be subjected to the sort of ambivalent parody that Linda Hutcheon [an American cultural critic] associates with postmodern textuality. These generic and tonal variations occur within scenes as well as across scenes, sometimes oscillating on a line-by-line basis, or across episodes when scenes set in paradigmatic relationship to one another(through the use of the same character, setting, or soundtrack music) are given virtually antithetical treatments. The movement in and out of parodic discourse is common in all of the episodes. For example, in the pilot, when Dale Cooper and Harry Truman are going through Laura Palmer's diary and personal effects, the dialogue, delivery, and soundtrack music all operate according to the conventions of the Jack Webb police procedural. But the 'just the facts, ma'am' tone of Cooper's discourse about cocaine, safety deposit boxes, and court orders is shattered by the concluding line of the scene, which is delivered in exactly the same manner: 'Diane, I'm holding in my hand a box of chocolate bunnies.'

[...]

It could be argued that this tonal oscillation and generic amalgamation, in which viewers are encouraged to activate ever-shifting sets of expectations and decoding strategies, is simply one of those 'Lynchian tricks' – that in *Twin Peaks*, as in *Blue Velvet* [an earlier film of his], Lynch labors to catch his viewers *between* sets of expectations, producing the shock of the newly juxtaposed.

Although this oscillation in tonality is undeniably a characteristic of Lynch's more recent projects, it is also reflective of changes in television entertainment and of viewer involvement in that entertainment. That viewers would take a great deal of pleasure in this oscillation and juxtaposition is symptomatic of the 'suspended' nature of viewer involvement in television that developed well before the arrival of *Twin Peaks*. The ongoing oscillation in discursive register and generic conventions describes not just *Twin Peaks* but the very act of moving up and down the television scale of the cable box. While watching *Twin Peaks,* viewers may be overtly encouraged to move in and out of an ironic position, but watching other television soap operas (nighttime or daytime) involves for many viewers a similar process of oscillation in which emotional involvement alternates with ironic detachment. Viewing perspectives are no longer mutually exclusive, but set in perpetual alternation.

What distinguishes *Twin Peaks* from, say, *Dallas* or *Knots Landing* [1980s US soaps] is not that it encourages this alternation in viewing positions but that it explicitly acknowledges this oscillation and the suspended nature of television viewing. In other words, *Twin Peaks* doesn't just acknowledge the multiple subject positions that television generates; it recognizes that one of the great pleasures of the televisual text is that very suspension and exploits it for its own ends.

Reading source

Collins, 1992, pp.345–8 ■ ■ ■

From doing the activity for Reading 5.2 you will probably have started to reflect on just how great the difference is between Collins's postmodern approach to television and the 'big ideology' position developed by the mid-1970s, film theorists. Collins proposes that postmodern texts invite oscillation between viewing positions and a suspension of involvement. The film theorists, conversely, argued for centring (Baudry), or the fixing of subject position via that hierarchy of discourses found in the classic realist text (McCabe).

Significantly, postmodernism has now been digested by media studies. Textual analysts, at the beginning of the twenty-first century, rarely use the term. Yet many have absorbed the concepts associated with it. So, the notion of media texts as being fluid, in other words offering different subject positions, remains important; so too does the theme of intertextuality (see Chapter 2, Section 5). More generally, the acceptance in postmodernism that the world of the text has replaced a social reality beyond the text is now widespread. We might say that the turn to postmodernism has helped to bring constructionist ideas into the mainstream of academic thinking, and even into the world beyond.

Parody, intertextuality and hybridity are, of course, all ways in which texts refer to other texts. It could, then, be argued that it is perfectly correct to focus on these themes because media texts now embody them to a much greater extent than before. This was the historical side of the argument about postmodernism: media culture has become much more reflexive, much more concerned with itself. Textual analysis ought therefore to investigate the phenomenon. As we discussed in the introduction to this chapter, the rise of celebrity might be considered to encapsulate such a trend. In a celebrity culture the reference point of media texts becomes the production of fame, or the making of people into texts. In this context a genre such as 'reality TV' is not concerned with revealing reality so much as importing it (namely ordinary people and situations), and then transforming that reality.

Yet it is by no means clear whether such constructionism from *within* the media is actually in the ascendant. Realism continues alongside parody and hybridity, or even incorporates them, as we saw in the case of *The Royle Family*. And if it were to be shown that intertextuality is the predominant trend in the contemporary period, this would not necessarily be a good reason for textual analysis to adopt a constructionist position. It could be argued that the new media forms are ideological and that they obscure reality in the interests of power, even if they do this in very different ways than were proposed for the classic realist text.

It seems, then, that while constructionism is the major tendency in textual analysis it is by no means the only 'show in town' and that other, more critical, approaches are possible in the contemporary period. For a discussion of one such approach to news reporting and factual media genres – critical discourse analysis – see Chapter 4, Section 2.

5   Conclusion

Over the course of this chapter we have examined three broad positions concerning the relationship of media texts to the world: realism, ideological analysis and constructionism. In terms of the three themes which organise this book we can note the following.

Each of the broad positions is strongly engaged with the question of power and its intimate connection to knowledge, values and belief. What distinguishes the positions in the first instance is *where* each locates power. In realism, power is an aspect of social relations. The most powerful groups in society (the bourgeoisie, men, white people and heterosexuals, for example) ensure a social order which reflects their interests and ensures their continuing power over the less powerful. Realist critics and media producers not only want to produce knowledge of this world, they generally hold to a critical system of values and belief; that is, they want to show social reality in media texts so that the world might be changed, either by reform or revolution. Of course, this is not the exclusive concern of realism. Its practitioners tend to want their texts to be beautiful, moving and stylish too. Still, realism must by definition have social reality, and the power which underpins it, in its sights. And that means beautiful, moving and stylish may sometimes be qualities to avoid. Brecht, for instance, advocates shock tactics as a way of breaking out of conventional means of representation that have become a barrier to accessing the real.

For ideological analysis the task is to show how power operates at the level of ideas. In the original Marxist conception of ideology dominant ideas represent the dominant class and its interests. From this perspective, analysis of ideology should show how media texts carry those embedded assumptions which naturalise or legitimate social relations. In other words, this is a realist approach which examines how texts may systematically cover up the real. However, in the Althusserian view of ideology which became dominant in film and media studies in the 1970s, ideology and the texts which embody it are thought to be the *source* of power as well as being powerful in their effects. As a result social reality almost disappears from view. With this move comes a strong scepticism towards the possibility of knowledge, or even the existence, of the real. Indeed, realist texts are treated with the most suspicion precisely because of their misleading claim to be able to convey reality. As regards values and beliefs, textual analysis in what we have been calling the 'big ideology' school still has a critical edge. It operates on the basis that dominant social relations ought to be changed. But since these can hardly be discerned it expects to be able to do little more than show ideological processes at work in the media.

Constructionism, then, adopts the text-oriented concept of power at stake in 'big ideology', while repudiating its one-dimensionality. Texts may be relatively open and enable different subject positions to be taken, sometimes in the same text (see Reading 5.2). But now, and crucially, there is no hard and fast distinction between texts and the world. All knowledge is textual in the sense that there is nothing that can be known beyond language and signs. As for the values and beliefs which inform analysis, these are, once again, critical in their thrust. Yet, since social reality has in effect been 'pulled up' into the text, it is now possible to right wrongs at the level of the text – through analysis itself. Thus, for example, feminist criticism may show how women are empowered in soap operas. We surveyed some other examples of this redemptive textual politics in Section 1.

Finally, what of continuity and change? At the level of approaches to textual analysis we have seen considerable change, from realism as the dominant paradigm, through ideological critique, to constructionism in the contemporary period. It would be dangerous to oversimplify, however. In practice there is plenty of textual analysis today which draws on more than one of these positions. And, if realism is in the shade at the moment, then (a realist might argue) changes in social reality will surely bring it back to the fore.

DVD-ROM

Now that you have finished reading Chapter 5, work through the Politics of Representation activities in the Chapter Activities area of the DVD-ROM, *Analysing Media Texts*. ■ ■ ■

Further reading

Kirkham, P. and Skeggs, B. (1999) '*Absolutely Fabulous*: Absolutely Feminist?' in Geraghty, C. and Lusted, D. (eds) *The Television Studies Book*, London, Arnold. This is an interesting example of constructionist criticism which suggests that television texts have become increasingly concerned with their own status as texts. It also refers to the 'male gaze'; see Mulvey (1993) below.

Mulvey, L. (1993) 'Visual pleasure and narrative cinema', in Easthope, A. (ed.) *Contemporary Film Theory*, London, Longman. A classic and highly influential essay, this is a strong version of the ideological critique found in British film studies of the 1970s, but oriented towards questions of sex and gender.

Roberts, J. (1998) *The Art of Interruption: Realism, Photography and the Everyday*, Manchester, Manchester University Press. Realist criticism at quite an advanced level – and dealing with photography. It is to be recommended because it is one of the few books that defends realism in the light of constructionist arguments; see especially the Introduction.

References

Adorno, T., Benjamin, W., Bloch, E., Brecht, B. and Lukács, G. (1980) *Aesthetics and Politics*, London, Verso.

Althusser, L. (1971) 'Ideology and ideological state apparatuses' in *Lenin and Philosophy, and Other Essays* (trans. and ed. B. Brewster), London, New Left Books.

Barthes, R. (1977) 'The photographic message' in *Image, Music, Text* (trans. S. Heath), London, Fontana.

Baudry, J-L. (1992/1975) 'Ideological effects of the basic cinematographic apparatus' in Mast, G., Cohen, M. and Braudy, L. (eds) *Film Theory and Criticism* (4th edn), New York, Oxford University Press.

Collins, J. (1992) 'Television and postmodernism' in Allen, R. (ed.) *Channels of Discourse, Reassembled* (2nd edn), London, Routledge.

Evans, J. and Hesmondhalgh, D. (2005) *Understanding Media: Inside Celebrity*, Maidenhead, Open University Press/The Open University (Book 1 in this series).

Hall, S. (1997/1974) 'The television discourse – encoding and decoding' in Gray, A. and McGuigan, J. (eds) *Studying Culture: An Introductory Reader* (2nd edn), London, Arnold.

Hill, J. (1986) *Sex, Class and Realism: British Cinema 1956–1963*, London, British Film Institute.

Lukács, G. (1972/1950) *Studies in European Realism* (trans. Edith Bone), London, The Merlin Press.

Marx, K. (2004/1932) *The German Ideology*, vol.1, part 1, section B, Marx/Engles Internet Archive (marxists.org), www.marxists.org/archive/marx/works/1845/german-ideology/ch01b.htm (accessed 13 December 2004).

McCabe, C. (1981/1974) 'Realism and the cinema: notes on some Brechtian theses' in Bennett, T., Boyd-Bowman, S., Mercer, C. and Woollacott, J. (eds) *Popular Television and Film*, London, British Film Institute.

Tagg, J. (1988) *The Burden of Representation*, Amherst, MA, University of Massachusetts Press.

Thompson, J. (1990) *Ideology and Modern Culture*, Cambridge, Polity Press.

Zola, E. (1998/1885) *Germinal*, Oxford, Oxford Paperbacks.

Framing the real: beyond the text

Jason Toynbee and Marie Gillespie

As we have seen, three themes are intertwined throughout each of the chapters of this book. To recap, these are:

1   power

2   change and continuity

3   knowledge, values and beliefs.

This is not a random selection. The themes take us straight to key ways in which texts matter in the larger social world. If there is one question that crops up again and again in relation to textual analysis it is 'Why bother to do it?' For many starting out in media studies the task of minutely examining a popular (and to some, trivial) sitcom or photograph in a newspaper may seem arcane, or a waste of time. However, the analysis of media texts is central to understanding the ways in which meanings are organised and circulated in society. So what we shall do here is bring together and summarise some of the reasons already presented as to why the analysis of media texts matters very much indeed.

Power

Perhaps the most obvious way of thinking about power is in terms of 'power over'. Thus it frequently has been argued that media texts have the power to influence individuals and societies, even if the exact nature and degree of that influence is open to question. This perspective emerges most strongly in the last two chapters. The critical approach to discourse and content analysis presented by David Hesmondhalgh in Chapter 4 starts from the premise that texts often represent the world according to the interests of dominant groups in society. That is to say, media messages in general, and discourse in particular, tend to be partisan. Yet *how* they are partisan is not apparent. What critical discourse analysis does, like any approach which is suspicious of the ways in which power is embedded in media texts, is to 'unveil' the hidden subtexts of media. In the case of critical content analysis the influence of power relations operating in texts will be more obvious. These forms of analysis demonstrate the *extent* to which a particular, partisan view of the world is presented. The task is the enumeration of linguistic terms, themes and functions that typify and give semantic weight to that world view. The quantity, rather than the quality, of terms and functions provides the key to the terms used. Chapter 5, then, opens out the theme of power, showing how approaches to ideology in media studies, informed by Marxism but also feminism, have posited that everyday ways of understanding the world are systematically distorted or illusory in order to serve the interests of power. The role of the media is key here in naturalising common-sense ideas, from our very sense of self-hood (or subjectivity) to notions of racial hierarchy, which may be implicit in the way certain narratives are structured.

What we have discussed so far is a strong version of textual power, one in which dominant social groups (for example, men, white people, the bourgeoisie) have *power over* others, and in which this power is in turn projected through media texts – for instance, through the ways in which a news story may assume that the role of a mother is to stay at home and look after her baby. Another tendency in textual analysis, however, adopts a more diffuse conception of power. We can see this in Chapter 1 on semiotics, but it is also to be found in Chapters 2 and 3 on genre and narrative. Here, the codes and conventions by which texts operate impose limits on the nature of 'textuality' and of meaning. In effect, power emanates from the very structure of the text. The repetition of certain structures of meaning and feeling (as we have seen in the history of melodrama) is a fundamental way in which knowledge and hierarchies of value and status are reproduced. But, as we have seen, texts may also challenge dominant power relations (we look at this in the next section).

Finally, we can observe power as emerging from 'below' as a form of empowerment facilitated by media texts. Gill Branston and Marie Gillespie both suggest something along these lines when they point to the way in which genre and narrative are not simply structures, but can also be seen as processes that engage audiences and elicit their participation. Thus, the argument goes, the everyday textual analysis we do as lay members of an audience when we watch, listen, read and discuss has something democratic about it (see **Gillespie, 2005**).

Change and continuity

Media texts, it seems, are prone to constant transformations in form and content: the media depend on novelty and especially on innovations in style.

It is tempting to go no further than this, in other words to orient the discussion towards change and to downplay continuity. That is certainly a popular view. From at least the beginning of the twentieth century, systems of mass communications have been treated as emblems of modernity and innovation. Yet the apparently fast-changing domain of the media is actually given to a considerable degree of continuity. Things stay the same much more than we might imagine, and what appears to be change may sometimes mask underlying continuities.

With this warning in mind, we can look more critically at change in media texts. As Gill Branston points out in Chapter 2, intertextual combination, or hybridity, is one of the main ways in which new patterns of textual organisation, and ultimately new genres, emerge. Drawing on Janet Staiger's work, she argues that what defines hybrid work is its composition from genuinely distinct elements, and its more or less explicit challenge to existing power relations. One example Branston gives is the Cuban film *Oración*, which criticises US consumerism and imperialism by juxtaposing images that are normally kept separate: news footage of war, a Marilyn Monroe press conference, and so on. It might be said that *Oración* belongs to a new genre of 'photo-essay'. Yet this is hardly a genre as outlined in the chapter. Quite simply, it has not been taken up by the mainstream media industry and, as a consequence, has never been subject to repetitive industrial production and marketing.

Meanwhile, according to Staiger, what appear to be 'new' genres in cinema (say comic-horror) are the result of 'inbreeding' within a closed Hollywood genre-pool, rather than genuine hybridity. As such they are not really innovative at all. As Staiger argues, what we see in mainstream cinema is actually considerable continuity in terms of form and content over the long period of the Hollywood studio system, beginning in the 1920s and persisting today. Whether or not one agrees with Staiger about this history, there is an important general point to be made. Textual analysis that seeks to identify an emerging style or new themes ought to be done with caution. Banal structural continuity often lies behind dramatic surface change, and it is worth considering this every time we encounter the announcement of a brave new genre or stylistic departure.

Knowledge, values and beliefs

Reflection on knowledge, values and beliefs pretty much saturates this book. Take narrative: as Marie Gillespie shows, storytelling involves the controlled release of knowledge via the plot, and then, on the part of the audience, the construction of a coherent story from what is revealed. But this is not an automatic process. The key point is that narratives are puzzles. They depend on constant problem solving by the listener, reader or spectator. All narratives, we might say, have as a meta-plot the theme of how to find things out, and this is as true in a melodrama like *Imitation of Life* as it is in a detective story, even if in the former case we are finding out about characters and their relationships rather than who killed whom.

So far, we have what seems like a fairly value-neutral account of the revelation of knowledge in narratives. But when we consider the range and depth of knowledge that we are offered by a particular text – for example, the degree of access we gain into a character's knowledge and emotional state – then questions of value obviously enter the picture. In taking the audience into the 'heart and mind' of a character, narratives privilege certain ways of looking at the story world. More than this, if the narrative is competent, the audience identifies with the character to the extent of *believing* in or with her or him, even while knowing very well that all such belief is summoned up by the narrative process.

This 'suspension of disbelief', as it is sometimes called, is a remarkable aspect of the power of storytelling. It helps to explain why ideological critique of film during the 1970s focused so strongly on narrative. But how, given this illusionism, can realists think that stories are capable of showing truths about society; truths not merely about its appearance but about its underlying structure too? The answer (discussed in Chapter 5) is that through the development of story and character, fiction may show the social world with a particular intensity and aptness, as in the case, perhaps, of British social realist films of the 1960s. Instead of focusing on the way one is 'taken in' by the story, as ideological critique suggests, realists point to the way in which narratives present real situations.

Reflecting on realism brings us back to a central argument about knowledge, values and beliefs. This is whether media texts, and the signifying systems that underpin them, are *ever* capable of a realistic portrayal of the world. The issue is not merely to do with the tendency of, for example, narrative form to make us suspend disbelief in a fictional world. It bears more fundamentally on the nature of knowledge.

Realists consider that things exist independently of language or other signifying systems, and that we get to know them by means of signification. Constructionists, on the other hand, argue that all that we know is produced through codes and conventions, and nothing can be said to exist except in the shape-forming means of signification. This, of course, takes us back to Chapter 1 on semiotics. As Jostein Gripsrud shows, semiotics poses the priority of the signifier over the signified. Indeed, it is the structure of the differences between signifiers that produces the signified. Ultimately, the word 'dog' summons up the concept of dog because 'dog' is not 'cat', not 'bog', not 'wolf', and so on and so forth.

Constructionism of this kind is, if pursued to its logical conclusion, incompatible with realism. To treat texts as though they are capable of revealing the real world beyond the text (the realist approach), is to do something fundamentally different from considering that texts construct the world (the constructionist approach). As in all areas of the humanities and social sciences, there is a disagreement here, and this is one of the important, if frustrating, things we hope you will take away from this book.

In the end, though, textual analysis is worth doing because mediated meanings and pleasures are everywhere. In industrial societies we live immersed in media. Textual analysis helps us to make sense of this phenomenon.

Reference

Gillespie, M. (ed.) (2005) *Media Audiences*, Maidenhead, Open University Press/The Open University (Book 2 in this series).

DVD-ROM

Now go to the DVD and work your way through the final activity – the Sequence Builder. This is where we hand over to you and you become a storyteller as well as a media analyst. You can build your own sequence of stills with dialogue, music and sound effects. It is serious fun and enables you to bring together all that you have learned through the five chapters of this book. Have fun! ■ ■ ■

Acknowledgements

Grateful acknowledgement is made to the following sources for permission to reproduce material within this book.

Chapter 1

Figures

Figure 1.1: Copyright © BBC Television; Figure 1.4 (a): Copyright © Redferns Music Picture Library; Figure 1.4 (b): Copyright © Allastair Grant/AP/Empics; Figure 1.5: Copyright © Joseph Sohm; Visions of America/Corbis; Figure 1.7: Copyright © MGM/The Kobal Collection/ Clarence Sinclair Bull; Figure 1.9 (a): Copyright © BBC Photo Library; Figure 1.9 (b): Copyright © ITV Granada; Figure 1.9 (c): Copyright © Lorimar/The Kobal Collection; Figure 1.9 (d): Spelling/The Kobal Collection; Figure 1.11: Perrie, R. (2004) 'School health warning: conkers may shatter when hit by another conker', *The Sun*, 4 October 2004. Copyright © News International. Main photo copyright © Louise Porter; Figure 1.12: Copyright © Action Images; Figure 1.13: Copyright © AP/AP/Empics.

Chapter 2

Readings

Reading 2.1: taken from Staiger, J. (2003) 'Hybrid or inbred: the purity hypothesis and Hollywood genre history', in Grant, B.K. (ed.) *Film Genre Reader III*, University of Texas Press; Reading 2.2: Williams, L. (1998) 'Melodrama revisited', in Browne, N. (ed.) *Refiguring American Film Genres: History And Theory*, University of California Press. By courtesy of Linda Williams.

Figures

Figure 2.1: Copyright © Paramount Pictures/Ronald Grant Archive; Figure 2.2: Copyright © Icon Entertainment/Ronald Grant Archive; Figure 2.3: Copyright © HBO/The Kobal Collection/Anthony Neste; Figure 2.4: Copyright © Eros International/Ronald Grant Archive; Figure 2.5: Copyright © Universal; Figure 2.6: Copyright © BBC Photo Library; Figure 2.7: Copyright © Steve Bell 2001; Figure 2.8: Copyright © Bend It Films/Ronald Grant Archive; Figure 2.10: Copyright © Dreamworks SKG/Ronald Grant Archive; Figure 2.11: Copyright © United Artists/The Kobal Collection; Figure 2.12: Copyright © Associated Press/APTN/Empics.

Chapter 3

Reading

Reading 3.2: Gibbs, J. (2002) *Mise-en-Scène: Film Style and Interpretation*, Wallflower Press.

Figures

Figure 3.1 (a): AKG-Images; Figure 3.1 (b): Copyright © MGM/Ronald Grant Archive; Figure 3.1 (c): Ronald Grant Archive; Figure 3.2: Copyright © Josef Scaylea/Corbis; Figure 3.3: Bridgeman Art Library; Figure 3.4: Copyright © Universal; Figure 3.6: Copyright © Universal; Figure 3.8: The Art Archive/Bibliotheque des Arts Decoratifs Paris/Dagli Orti; Figure 3.9: Copyright © Paramount Pictures/Roanld Grant Archive; Figure 3.10: Copyright © Universal; Figure 3.11: Copyright © Universal; Figure 3.12: Copyright © Universal.

Chapter 4

Readings

Reading 4.1: Fairclough, N. (1995) *Media Discourse*, Edward Arnold. Copyright © 1995 Norman Fairclough. Reproduced by permission of Edward Arnold; Reading 4.2: Van Dijk, T.A. (2000) 'News(s), racism: a discourse analytical approach', in Cottle, S. (ed.) *Ethnic Minorities and the Media: Changing Cultural Boundaries.* Reproduced by kind permission of Open University Press/McGraw-Hill Publishing Company.

Figures

Figure 4.1: Kay, J. and Bowyer, A. (1989) 'Britain invaded by an army of illegals', *The Sun*, 2 February 1989. Copyright © News International; Figure 4.3: Copyright © EDPICCS/Mathew Usher/Rex Features.

Chapter 5

Figures

Figure 5.1: Canal+ Image UK; Figure 5.2: Canal+ Image UK; Figure 5.3: Copyright © BBC; Figure 5.4: Copyright © Ed Holub/Photonica/Getty Images.

Every effort has been made to contact copyright holders. If any have been inadvertently overlooked the publishers will be pleased to make the necessary arrangements at the first opportunity.

Index

What to do with the DVD

Insert the disk into the DVD drive on your computer. A dialogue box will appear. Double-click on 'Install' to start the installation and follow the instructions as they appear. You will be left with an icon on your desktop labelled 'Analysing Media Texts'. Double-click on this to run the software. The disk must be in the DVD drive when using the software, even after installation.

If the installation program doesn't start automatically, click on the 'Start' menu and then click 'Run...'. Type in <drive>:/install.exe, where <drive> is the letter of your DVD drive: for example, D:/install.exe.

You will need to have Macromedia Flash and Adobe Reader installed to use this DVD-ROM.